VICO MAGISTRETTI

VICO MAGISTRETTI

DESIGNER

Text and catalogue by Vanni Pasca

Art Director: Italo Lupi

RIZZOLI
NEW YORK

First published in the United
States of America in 1991 by
RIZZOLI INTERNATIONAL
PUBLICATIONS, INC.
300 Park Avenue South
New York, NY 10010

Library of Congress Cataloging-in-Publication Data

Pasca, Vanni.
[Vico Magistretti, L'eleganza della ragione. English]
Vico Magistretti, designer/Vanni Pasca.
    p. cm.
Translation of: Vico Magistretti, L'eleganza della ragione.
Includes bibliographical references.
ISBN 0-8478-1342-8 (pbk.)
1. Magistretti Vico, 1920– — Criticism and interpretation.
2. Furniture design — Italy—History—20th century. I. Title.
NK2562.M34V513 1991
749.25—dc20
                                        90-50853
                                        CIP

Editorial conception: Passigli Progetti, Milan
English translation: Kate Singleton

Art Director: Italo Lupi
Graphic designer: Alessandro Farina

Photographic Sources
Aldo Ballo, Gabriele Basilico,
Santi Caleca, Mario Carrieri,
Casali, Carla De Benedetti,
Fortunati, Foto Dani,
Yukio Futagawa, Ugo Mulas,
Novelli Film, Rotalfoto,
G. Sinigaglia, Luciano Soave,
Studio Monti, Studio 22,
Yukio Takase.

Printed and bound in Italy

Contents

SKETCHING: MY SEARCH FOR INSIGHT

To Stefano,
Susanna
Margherita and
Bartolomeo.

The editors of this book on my work felt it would
be a good idea to accompany the pictures with
reproductions of sketches and drawings that I have
made over the years. I imagine that they've done
this not because I draw particularly well, but
because they believed that this would be a way of
illustrating how I work, and what I see as the
difference between Sketching and Design.
When I hold conferences or give lessons, I always
try to explain that the work of the designer should
not get too tied up in minute definitions of all
aspects of every detail.
I have always felt that design, at least as far as my
experience in Italy is concerned, is the outcome of
close collaboration between the manufacturer and
the designer. The task of the designer is to come
up with the design concept — the overall sense of
the image and use of each project — and rely on
the sophisticated technical ability of the
manufacturer as far as the design's realization is
concerned. Design objects are not born on the
drawing board, but come into being where they
are actually produced, in a continual exchange of
observations and suggestions.
In this sense, all the sketches in the book try to
bear witness to the way my design drawings, from
their earliest stages, try to illustrate not so much
the image as the meaning of the objects. At the
same time they suggest the technical means and
the materials necessary for economic and
appropriate mass production. Drawing for me
doesn't mean reproducing the object in all its
morphological and technical aspects. Rather, it
means digging down to ever greater depths in
search of the very essence of the object, looking at
usual things with an unusual eye.
This is what design is for me. And sketching is
what expresses it.
"Ceci n'est pas une pipe," wrote Magritte as a
title for a painting portraying a pipe. In design,
too, behind the pipe, if you look hard enough you
may find something else.

Vico Magistretti

VICO MAGISTRETTI: THE ELEGANCE OF REASON

Vico Magistretti is well known as a designer, both in Italy and throughout the world; his work constitutes one of the most significant contributions to the international success of Italian design. Magistretti's initial group of designs toward the end of the forties was followed by a decade largely dedicated to architecture. In the late fifties he returned to design work and has been going strong ever since. Even in recent times, when the neo-avant-garde design of the early eighties seems to have been heading downhill, a number of Magistretti's furniture designs have drawn considerable attention for their innovative thinking.

Magistretti has designed objects that have become bestsellers but at the same time, he has won innumerable awards, has had his work selected for the permanent collections of museums in sever-

al countries (the Museum of Modern Art in New York holds twelve of his designs), and has been the object of constant attention on the part of design critics and historians. Both communicative and thoughtful, readily accessible and intellectually stimulating, Magistretti's designs manage to combine popular success and cultural significance.

This characteristic is shared by a number of designers who have made fundamental contributions to the development of Italian design: Castiglioni and Marco Zanuso, for instance. But then Italian furniture design as a whole, despite its various trends and individuals, has always made its mark both commercially and culturally.

Magistretti has worked almost exclusively as a furniture designer,

Torre Parco in via Revere, Milan (with F. Longoni), 1956.

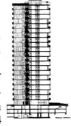

rarely turning his attention elsewhere. For this reason, the term "design" here will refer mainly to furniture design, a point worth making for at least two reasons.

First and foremost, furniture has always been a major focus of Italian design, whose international renown indeed largely depends on products of this sort. And second, a unitary definition of design no longer appears to be feasible. As far back as 1974 Tomás Maldonado could write that "industry as an abstract, monolithic entity was a myth of the nineteenth century. What really exist are industries in the plural. For this same reason there is no one industrial design, but rather a number of them, all quite different from each other. The monistic concept of industrial design should thus be replaced by a pluralistic one."[1]

Like most Italian designers Magistretti was trained as an architect, and throughout his career he has designed buildings as well as objects. This biographical fact does not imply that Magistretti — like many of his colleagues during the eighties — has tended to introduce architectural images into his interiors.

If for the most part the cultures of design and architecture have coincided in Italy, it is not least because they share a critical revision of the form of rationalism that developed there in the fifties, a dialogue that also informs Magistretti's approach to design, in which the language of rationalism is softened to achieve an elegant balance between modernity and memory.

Magistretti's work reveals a strong continuity of approach; yet this does not mean that he is insensitive to the evolution of tastes

Studies for lamps, c. 1984.

Pages 12-13: The Arosio Villa at Arenzano, 1959.

and behavior, or unaware of the problems that at one time or another have concerned the design world. Indeed he has always been ready to try out new materials, to take on new challenges, and to work out new solutions. But Magistretti's approach to design and to form has been singularly consistent; cultural, technical, and behavioral changes have been quietly absorbed into his overall system over the years, without giving rise to mannerisms of any sort. Thus we might more effectively examine Magistretti's work in terms of its different themes — moving from an analysis of particular objects to an understanding of overall approach — than by proceeding in blandly chronological terms. Such a portrait of the designer is bound to bring into focus a series of traits that have been typical of Italian design as a whole from its

earliest stages in the thirties, through the influential fifties, and beyond to a present in which Italian design has achieved a distinctive and universal identity of its own.

The expression "Italian design" has hitherto been used to refer to a specific entity. The critic R. De Fusco, pointing out that critics and historians have "tried to establish definitions of design which have later proved to be inconsistent with the facts," suggests that it would be better to "describe how design manifests itself," rather than to attempt to "say what design is."[2]

At base, this proposal probably draws from the empiricism informing Bridgeman's "operative criticism."[3] Granted, this too has come in for some discussion, but in the present situation, with its lack of universally accepted concepts — or indeed, as far

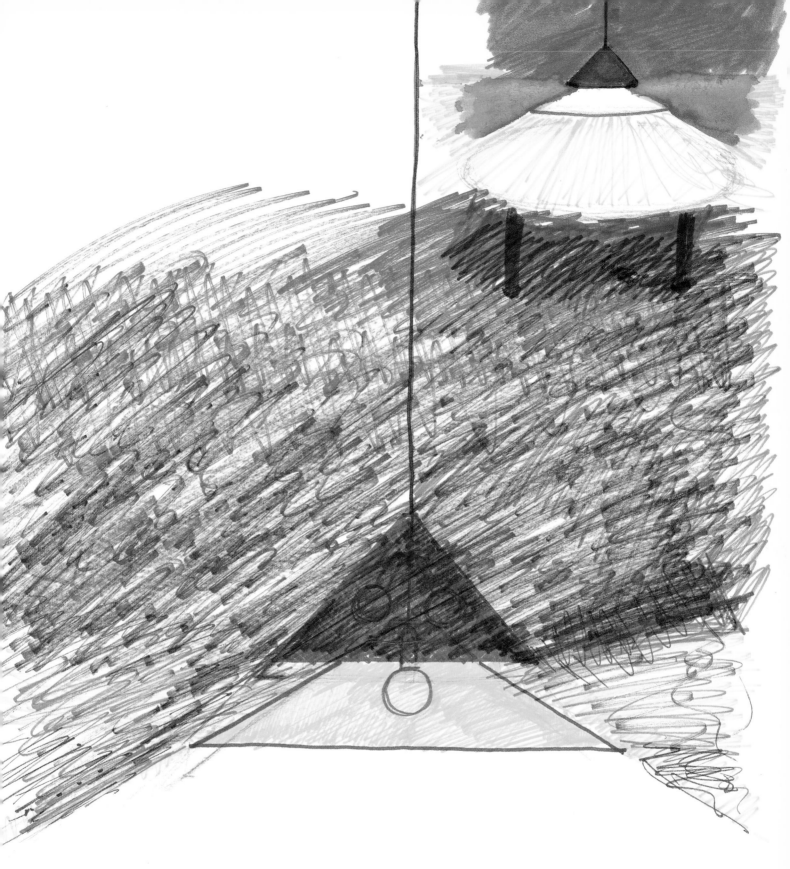

as design is concerned, coherent ones (suffice it to recall the different types of design already mentioned) — De Fusco's proposal may be useful in stimulating concrete analysis and avoiding misunderstandings. Thus we will analyze Magistretti's work here within the context of Italian design, with the aim of contributing to a deeper understanding of both phenomena.

1. T. Maldonado, Avanguardia e razionalità (Turin, 1974), p. 144. More recently, other authors have pointed out that each of the various sectors of design calls for individual treatment that can take into account the different degrees of technological complexity, planning, production and distribution. Cf. R. Zorzi, "Forma come comunicazione," Alfabeta, September 1986, no. 88.
2. R. De Fusco, Storia del design (Milan, 1985), p. vii.
3. Percy William Bridgman (1882–1961), the American physicist and philosopher of science, proposed a theory regarding the definition of scientific concepts that has also influenced sociologists and psychologists. According to this theory, all absolute concepts should be eliminated, in so far as they are meaningless or merely verbal. All physical concepts should thus be defined in terms of operations that can be carried out empirically, such that their applicability to the case in question can be individually established.

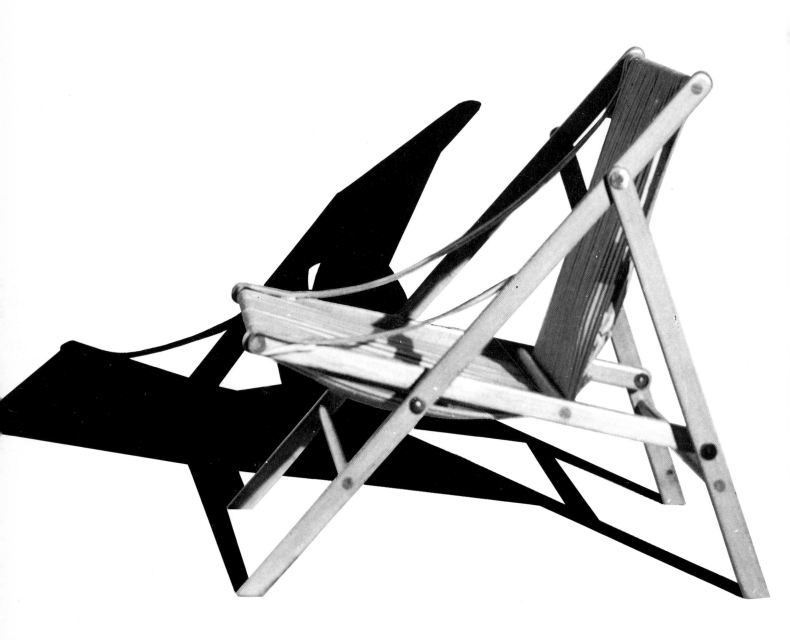

THE FIFTIES BETWEEN ARCHITECTURE AND DESIGN

The fifties are of fundamental importance for Italian design, and
for Magistretti's work in particular: during this decade certain
conditions begin to take shape and a number of themes come to
the fore. It thus seems appropriate to dedicate some initial attention to the period.
Born in 1920, Magistretti thus belongs to an intermediate generation bridging the "masters of Modernism" of the thirties and the
later generation that comprises such names as Vittorio Gregotti
and Aldo Rossi. He took his degree in architecture in Milan in
1945, having studied at the Champ Universitaire Italien de
Lausanne, an institute attached to Lausanne University. Here,
along with other Italians such as Alberto Rosselli and Angelo
Mangiarotti, he followed Ernesto Nathan Rogers's course on the

Stackable wood tables. Produced by Azucena, 1946. Left: RIMA exhibition in Milan. Stackable canvas chair and bookcase with adjustable shelves, 1946.

theory of architecture and urban planning. The Italian Rogers was of Jewish origin, and during the Fascist period had been forced by the racial laws to accept anonymity, and later to expatriate. His influence over the architects of the fifties was considerable: Magistretti himself has acknowledged it in a number of interviews. He says of the Milanese architects, for instance, "We were all sons of the Modern Movement, that is of the BBPR practice ([Gianluigi] Banfi, [Lodovico] Belgiojoso, [Enrico] Peressutti and Rogers), of [Franco] Albini, of [Ignazio] Gardella, of [Luigi] Figini and [Gino] Pollini, and of [Giuseppe] Pagano who died at Mathausen. We were a group that had come into contact with a person as enlightened as Ernesto Rogers, who opened your eyes not to architecture but to culture."[1]

In 1946 Magistretti took part in the RIMA (Riunione Italiana per le Mostre di Arredamento, or Italian Furniture Show Reunion) exhibition in the *Triennale* building, truly the high temple of innovation for Italian architecture of the thirties. The theme of the exhibition was popular furnishing;[2] among the objects Magistretti designed for it were a bookcase whose shelves could be slid along two supports in metal tubing, connected by pressure to the ceiling and the floor[3] and a simple deck chair, a redesign in more elegant terms of the traditional model.

Later, in 1949, Magistretti, along with Castiglioni, Zanuso, Gardella, Albini, and others, took part in a show organized by Fede Cheti. This time his designs consisted of small stackable tables and a bookcase conceived like a ladder to be leant against

17

RIMA exhibition in Milan: folding
armchair and bookcase, 1946.

the wall. The tables were put into production by Azucena, a small company founded in 1949 by Luigi Caccia Dominioni and Ignazio Gardella, architects very close to Magistretti. Highly effective in their deliberate clarity and simplicity, these, as well as a table designed for Tecno,[4] were shortlisted for the Compasso d'Oro award in 1954. Although the table is perhaps a little redundant, the other furniture speaks for an adhesion to rationalism and a respect for craftmanship in production. Magistretti's lifelong interest in simple traditional objects unspoilt by conceptions of style is already evident in objects conceived for other purposes, such as the ladder that becomes a bookcase, or in those easily and efficiently transformed, like the traditional deck-chair. Both bear witness to an overt desire for simplicity, for modest understatement; in so doing they express not only an obvious rejection of the preponderant reproduction period furniture of the time, but also of the elaborate refinement of the Novecento style. Granted, a taste for simplicity had found a place in the culture of the time: "The civilized man embodies the principle of simplicity; this is particularly the case with the artist, that most civilized of civilized men," wrote Alberto Savinio in 1946.[5]

We have mentioned the firm Azucena, and the question calls for a little further analysis. The fifties witnessed the battle in support of the Modern Movement, with all its ethical and aesthetic implications, in the face of a growing awareness that this same Modern Movement was intrinsically schematic, appearing to have reached a point of no return with the International Style.

It was thus necessary to breathe fresh life into the Modern Movement by creating new paradigms and overcoming current limitations. Since the thirties this had meant opening up new fields of interplay, such as the relationship between modernity and tradition in architecture. In turn this led to an examination of the break with history brought about by the avant-garde movements. Alongside this "rehabilitation of the past," considerable interest grew in relating new architecture to its surrounding context, both the built environment and the natural one. Moreover, by built environment the young architects of the time meant not only historic edifices, but also anonymous buildings — immune to stylistic dictates and to the norms of historical eclecticism —, that had appeared over the course of time. As F. Irace has rightly

put it, "raising the question of the architectural heritage of a particular context indicates the desire to know and integrate with the environment — be it urban or domestic — and to reject the impulse for radical renewal in favor of gradual, effective reform."[6] And indeed, the heritage question concerns both architecture and furnishing, in that the "modern" should be introduced into a given context in such a way as to create dialogue rather than opposition.

At the time, it should be added, the Modern Movement as such comprised a number of positions. These ranged from attention to building and furnishing standards for low-cost housing (the theme of the so-called "Proletarian" *VIII Triennale*, held in 1947 at the height of postwar reconstruction) to the trend

represented by Azucena and similar firms, intent on producing quality furniture that could coexist with the antiques embellishing the apartments of the Milanese well-to-do. The modernity of such products is blended with echoes of select motifs from the past, in particular from the Lombard neoclassical tradition. As Belgiojoso wrote in 1946 about furnishing his own house, "Just as pleasant memories stay with us without upsetting our sense of life, so we have chosen to introduce certain elements of yesterday's house into today's, thus placing old furniture with new rather as memories coexist with thoughts."[7]

Ernesto Nathan Rogers helped to dispel the period's apparent contradiction of wishing to design low-cost popular furniture on the one hand and luxury items on the other: "individualist furni-ture made for the privileged few has helped and continues to help quicken the imagination and refine technique; current production takes on characteristics of its own, and yet embraces and develops from real experiences."[8] Rogers was central to the culture of design and architecture to which we have been referring, and to which Magistretti belonged. Another figure who greatly contributed to the liveliness and variety of this culture was Gio Ponti, whose multifaceted activities — embracing art, architecture and design as well as cultural organization and promotion — constitute a precedent for certain highly distinctive aspects of Italian design, including the world of Ettore Sottsass and Memphis.

The little furniture that Magistretti designed during the fifties

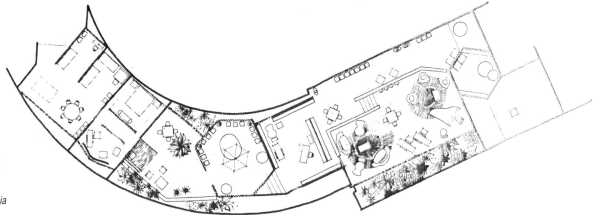

Pages 22-23: RIMA exhibition in Milan. The bookcase with tie-rods was designed by Magistretti; the rest of the furniture was produced by Moretti, 1946.

Exhibition of standard furniture, X Triennale, 1954, organized and displayed by Vico Magistretti (coordinating director), Luigi Caccia Dominioni and Mario Righini.

was for individual houses. Otherwise, he was engaged on two different fronts. The first was his involvement, along with other architects of the time, in research projects. These did not only consist of the famous *Triennale*,[9] in 1956 he joined the organizing committee that dealt with membership, rules, and cultural events of ADI, the Associazione per il Disegno Industriale (Italian Industrial Design Association). This body represented a fundamental moment of cohesion in the battle for the assertion of industrial design in Italy, paving the way for the acceptance of modern furniture as opposed to reproduction period furniture. In 1960 Magistretti joined Gardella and others on the board of the *XII Triennale*. Among the objects displayed were designs by Achille Castiglioni, Marco Zanuso, Tobia Scarpa, and Magis-

tretti himself, all of them witness to the mature professional capacity of designers able to relate to the nascent furniture industry.

Magistretti's main activity during the fifties, however, regarded architecture. His designs for an office building in corso Europa and for the Villa Arosio placed him at the forefront of new architecture in Milan. The Villa Arosio — presented at the eleventh CIAM congress held in Otterloo in 1959,[10] along with two other designs by Italian architects (the BBPR's Torre Velasca and Gardella's Olivetti Canteen at Ivrea) — elicited considerable discussion and some heated opposition from the upholders of orthodox modernism (for example, why adulterate the clarity of the plan with ''vernacular'' elements?); it represented that very

Left: Dining or gaming table,
designed for a Milan interior, 1946.

Wall-supported bookcase (1946),
exhibited in 1949 at the show
organized by Fedi Cheti.

revision of modernism that we have already mentioned.

In April of the same year Reyner Banham made a vehement attack on Italian architecture in an article entitled "Neoliberty: The Italian Retreat from Modern Architecture;" Rogers replied cuttingly in "The Evolution of Architecture: A Reply to the Refrigerator Keepers."[11] Both titles underline the reasons for the controversy explicity enough. In actual fact Italian culture in those years was dealing with subjects of great importance, many of them well in advance of later discussions developed within the realms of architecture both in Italy and elsewhere, as critics were ultimately to appreciate. In 1969 Oriol Bohigas declared that "despite the accusations that have been made, Milanese architecture in that period represented a real effort at maintaining con-

tinuity with authentic rationalism, even if those involved were in open disagreement with the meaningless formalisms to which the 'international style' had been reduced." In the same article Bohigas also refers to "the exemplary work of Magistretti who, although he did not get too involved in the theoretical formulations of the movement, was perhaps one of its most representative exponents as far as the number of achievements and his professional participation are concerned."[12]

By the end of the fifties, a new situation was beginning to emerge in Italy. The rules and realities of the economic boom had begun to show architects and designers that their aspirations to having a hand in directing the country's reconstruction were illusory. Designers found themselves in a situation that had undergone

Sending I, *extendible round table, Tecno, 1951.*

considerable change, and which called for professionals able to translate theories and earlier experiments into concrete proposals at a time when "chairs are no longer vestiges of culture, but rather commercial objects in the active sense of the word, links with the world of production."[13] Yet one of the basic aspects of Italian design culture remained unchanged. The political or utopian tensions of the previous period were transformed in the following years into the critical and rebellious design of the new generations, but the role of the designer as an autonomous entity able to communicate with industry on the basis of reciprocal respect was steadily upheld.

All those elements whose interaction shaped the development of Italian design in the following decades were already present by the end of the fifties.[14] First and foremost, the development that profoundly altered and modernized the country's socioeconomic situation — industrialization, the improvement in living standards, the expansion of consumption, urbanization and mass motorization — was in place. Second, furniture manufacture had been transformed from handicrafts to industry, with companies involved mostly small, or smallish, and tending to be both specialized and competitive. Last but not least, since the thirties the Italian architectural intelligentsia had been paying attention to home decorating and furniture. This interest can perhaps be partly explained in terms of a lack of other opportunities, and partly because design of this sort (and exhibition design, for that matter) has often proved to be fertile ground for experiments.

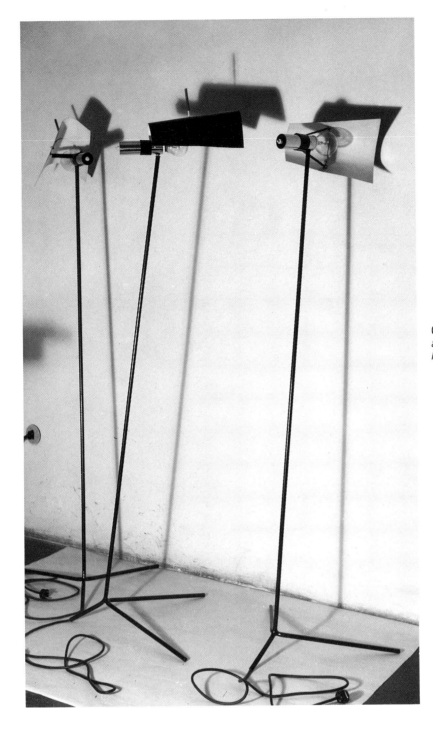

Claritas *lamp with metal rod shaft and sheet metal reflector (with Mario Tedeschi), 1946.*

However, the main reason for architecture's new involvement in furniture and interior design was quite simply the theoretical and moral importance attributed to the subject of living space on the part of architects of very different leanings, from Rogers to Ponti. In Rogers's words, "furniture design and town planning are the two extremes of the activity of a modern architect."[15]
Considered as an integral part of furnishing for the home, design became part of a system in which stylistic continuity is replaced by a continual effort to reinterpret history and the various typologies passed down by the experience of homemaking. And it is precisely in this that such developments in Italy differed from the design culture fostered by the Bauhaus or the Ulm school, both of which pursued "a universal social hygiene of forms"[16] based

on the technique and machinery that guarantee mass production and imbue a given age with particular formal qualities. Italian designers of the time could thus respond to manufacturer's interest in exploiting the transformation of lifestyles implicit in country's modernization. The demand for modern furniture could only grow, they avowed. And they were proved right: over the next few years Italian homes would change dramatically. Buying modern furniture became tantamount to adopting new habits and behavior, and the demand for the modern gradually came to overtake the traditional insistence on reproduction period furniture.[17]
Italian design thus derives from three basic elements: the country's transformation, the industrial production of furniture, and

27

design culture as such. The traits that were to characterize Italian design over the next few decades were the ability to promote technological innovation, the subsequent dynamism, and the almost excessive multiplication of models and images.[18]

In 1959 Vico Magistretti designed the clubhouse for the Carimate Golf Club at Carimate, just outside Milan. The furniture of the restaurant included the *Carimate* chair, an essential revisitation of the classic wooden country chair with a straw seat. This object may owe something to certain aspects of Scandinavian design (Kaare Klint, for example, often redesigned traditional wooden furniture to meet contemporary needs; another example of the same type of influence, in particular that of Finn Juhl, can be seen in the lathe-worked *Loden* armchair of 1961, another some-

what countrified design) that had been influential in a small way in Italy during the fifties. Yet the bright red gloss finish of the *Carimate* is highly individual.

In 1960 Magistretti met Cesare Cassina, one of the most dynamic members of that group of innovative manufacturers mentioned above. This encounter led to the industrial production of the *Carimate* chair in 1962, the beginning of a long-lasting, intense collaboration between the designer and the businessman.[19]

The *Carimate* chair — as in many other examples of Italian design, a mass-produced object designed by an architect for a particular environment — was the first of many successes. During the course of the sixties Magistretti designed other successful objects, in wood as well as plastic. A case in point is the *Selene*

Recreational Center at Rescaldina, 1956.

chair, which bears witness to the versatility that was to become the hallmark of Italian — and thus Milanese — design.[20] Magistretti was never inclined to launch into intricate theoretical disquisitions; his pragmatism has always led him to deal with different ideas, materials, and furniture types with equal ease. It is his overall approach to design that is unitary. In so being, it is also nonideological, as was that of Rogers before him: each case should be dealt with individually, for this is the only way to overcome the stultifying effects of "style." A rationalist by choice, Magistretti is therefore interested in mass production, yet his output embodies an elegance that proves immediately communicative and utterly individual — truly the answer to the user's aspirations.[21]

An effective definition of the quintessential Milanese designer was given a few years ago by E. Bonfanti: "We have spoken about the professionalism of the Milanese architects, but so general a term usually turns out to be inappropriate unless it is imbued with specific meaning. . . . The professional attitude has generally proved to be antiexperimental, slightly ahead of current architectural research, and able to fit in with many of the rules of the market. On the other hand, professional success, attained by means of high average quality, calls for keeping the average up. . . . Where someone like Magistretti (perhaps the best, in absolute terms, of the Milanese "professional" architects) is concerned, high standards of quality are a constant feature."[22]

29

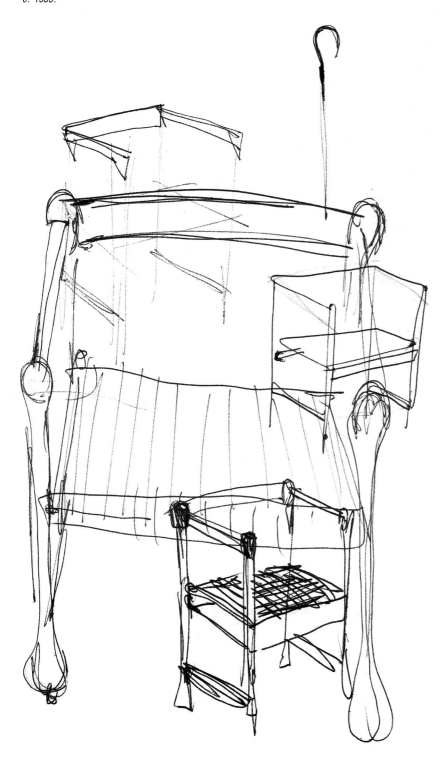

1. See the interview with Magistretti published in S. Giacomoni and A. Marcolli, Designer italiani *(Milan, 1988). The role played by Rogers can be further
clarified by quoting an architect who belongs to the generation following that
of Magistretti: Vittorio Gregotti refers to Rogers as "a personality who un-
doubtedly acted as the go-between linking the generation of the great masters
of modernism, who acted as an isolated avant-garde, and the critical awareness, the doubts and convictions that have characterized the best part of my
generation: and not only in Italy." V. Gregotti, "Ernesto Rogers,
1903–1969,"* Casabella, *no. 557 (May 1989).*
2. "Almost all the architects of the Modern Movement in Italy took part in
it," wrote Gregotti, "and the ideas proposed, especially on the part of the
younger generation, were both lively and enthusiastic. Flexibility, spatial
economy, and simplicity were the outstanding characteristics of the resulting
designs. Industrial awareness was almost nonexistent, and assembly was sim-

plified as far as possible. Yet the two seemed to balance each other out, such that the general outcome managed to be both internationally competitive and able to offer clients the chance (albeit perhaps in symbolic terms) of putting their own furnishing system together. The models that informed this offer belonged to the humble and largely unwritten history of tools and equipment: the deck chair, the folding table, simple, common items ennobled by the 'pride of modesty,' as expressed by Persico and the rationalists of the prewar period. Significant cases in point are the three-person home designed by Ignazio Gardella, the 'newlyweds' home by [Paolo] Chessa and [Vittoriano] Viganò, and the small, almost do-it-yourself items designed by Vico Magistretti, all of them devised and built for the RIMA." V. Gregotti, Il disegno del prodotto industriale. Italia 1860–1980 (Milan, 1982), p. 269.

3. This item may owe something to the bookcase designed by Carlo Scarpa during the late thirties. Although it was also fixed to the floor and ceiling, in terms of formal intent it was quite different, not least in view of the strongly characterized shelves. By contrast, Baroni suggests that Magistretti's design "recalls in particular the airy structures that Franco Albini had designed a few years earlier. Another point of reference might be Asplund's designs for the Stockholm Fair." D. Baroni, "Ludovico Magistretti" in Un'industria per il design, edited by M. Mastropietro (Milan, 1982), p. 227.

4. The table speaks for the presence of an industry that paid particular attention to structural solutions and mechanisms. It has a single-footed iron structure and a round wooden top. Two elements in the shape of a new moon, attached to the side of the table, can be swung up to increase the length, or down so that they act as a sort of vertical echo of the top.

5. Alberto Savinio, film review for Film Rivista, November 14, 1946.

6. F. Irace, "Il fascino discreto dell'architettura," Ottagono, no. 91 (December 1988).

7. L. Belgiojoso, "L'utile e gli antenati," Domus, no. 206 (February 1946).

8. E. N. Rogers, "Esperienze dell'ottava Triennale," Domus, no. 221 (July 1946).

9. In 1947 Magistretti was one of the curators of the Industrialized Building Show held as part of the VIII Triennale. At the IX Triennale in 1951, he organized with Mucchi the exhibition Architettura del lavoro (Building for Work). At the X Triennale in 1954 Magistretti, Caccia Dominioni, Gardella, and others were responsible for the Exhibition of Standards. Magistretti has been a member of the Centro Studi Triennale since 1958. See A. Pansera, Storia e cronaca della Triennale (Milan, 1978).

10. CIAM stands for Congrès Internationaux d'Architecture Moderne; the first took place in 1928, and the last at Otterloo in 1959, when it was decided to disband the organization. In reference to Magistretti's building designs of those years, Manfredo Tafuri writes, "The representative value of the image is a constant temptation for Italian architecture of the late fifties. In Milan this is present in the work of Vico Magistretti, an architect capable of creating unusual and striking volumetric compositions, as the Abeille Building goes to show." Tafuri, Storia dell'architettura italiana 1944–1985 (Turin, 1986), p. 87.

11. Banham's article appeared in Architectural Review, no. 747 (1959). Rogers answered in his editorial for Casabella-Continuità, no. 228 (1959).

12. O. Bohigas, "Aspetti già storici nell'opera di Vico Magistretti," Cuadernos de arquitectura, no. 72 (1969).

13. V. Gregotti, "Marco Zanuso, architetto della seconda generazione," Casabella, no. 216 (1957).

14. The success continued and increased during the eighties and up to the present. What is new today is the arrival on the furniture manufacturing scene of other countries, such as Spain; several designers from different countries (from Spain to France, Germany to Japan) have made a name for themselves, largely thanks to their discovery by Italian industries.

15. E. N. Rogers, "Henry Van De Velde o dell'evoluzione," Casabella-Continuità, no. 237 (1960).

16. G. Vattimo, La società trasparente (Milan, 1989), p. 90.

17. In 1968 in Italy "nearly 70% of consumption was covered by period furniture in the 'classic-traditional' style." Ten years later, "over 60% of the demand had moved over to 'modern' furniture, meaning furniture influenced by advanced design." Between 1973 and 1978, Italian furniture exports increased by 737%, in current lire, "whereas the ratio of the national product exported grows from 10% to 27%." S. Silvestrelli, Lo sviluppo industriale delle imprese produttrici di mobili in Italia (Milan, 1980), pp. 302–3, and p. 16.

18. For brevity we have neglected a fourth aspect of the question: the extraordinary capacity of Italian design and industry for promoting modern furniture by means of huge and articulated communications efforts such as the Compasso d'Oro, the Milan Furniture Salon, exhibitions, magazines, showrooms and so on.

19. In reference to the Maralunga sofa, Magistretti was the first to mention Cesare Cassina: "We worked together on it, both simultaneously grasping what it might turn out like, making the same gestures. A few minutes were enough for us to clinch the whole idea, and thus the object was born." P. C. Santini, Gli anni del design italiano — Ritratto di Cesare Cassina (Milan,

Studies for the clubhouse at the Carimate Golf Club, c. 1959.

Pages 32–33: Magistretti illustrates the location plan of the Milano S. Felice residential district, designed with Luigi Caccia Dominioni, 1965.

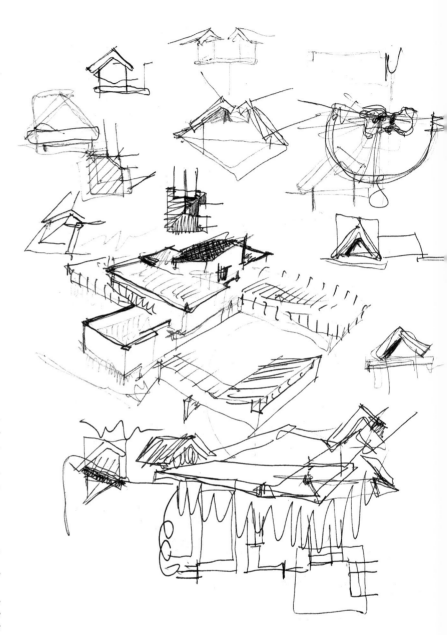

1981), p. 26.
Mention should also be made of the relationship with Francesco Binfaré, a gifted, eclectic collaborator and designer who worked for the firm.

20. This is a quintessentially Italian phenomenon: non-Italians are always amazed when they visit Magistretti's studio in Milan and discover it both to be small and to consist of just one collaborator, the draftsman Montella.

21. It should be added that "when Magistretti and others took part in the cultural debate of the reconstruction period they moved the focus of their interests from simplified architectural functionalism to a search for greater formal elegance, to the extent that they actually had much in common with the group of Milanese architects who had begun a process of revision of Rationalism." Baroni, "Ludovico Magistretti," p. 227.

22. E. Bonfanti, M. Porta, Città, Museo e Architettura (Florence, 1973), p. 166.

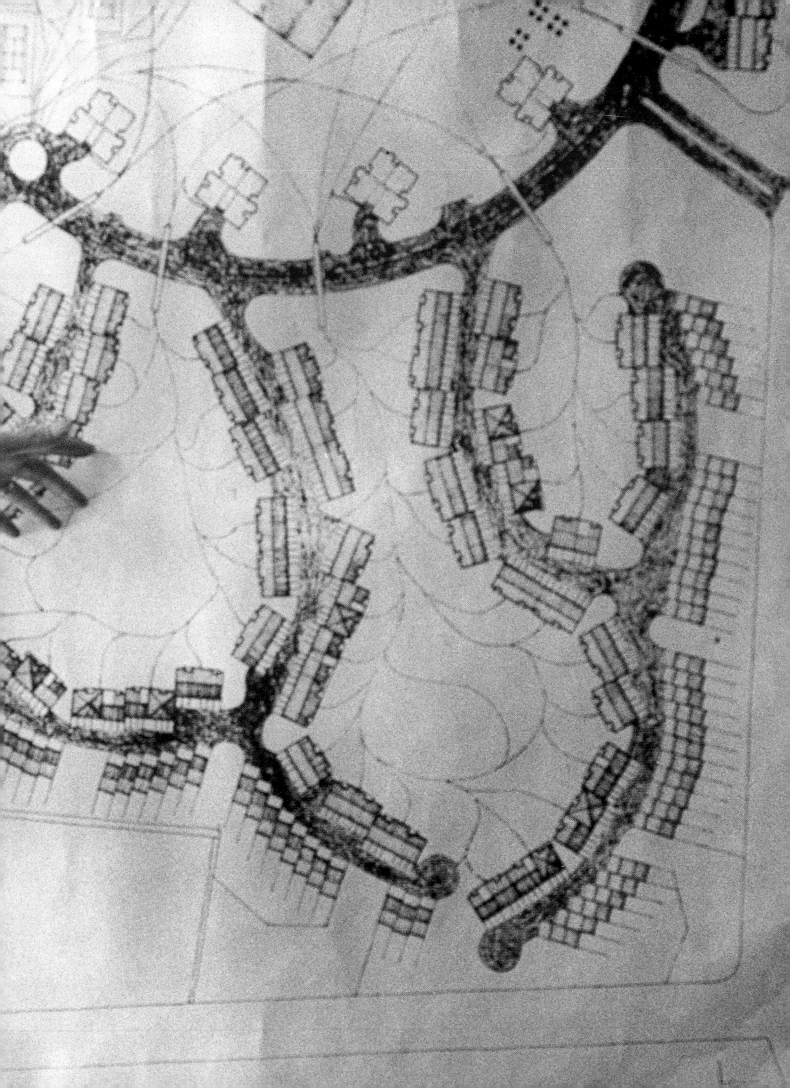

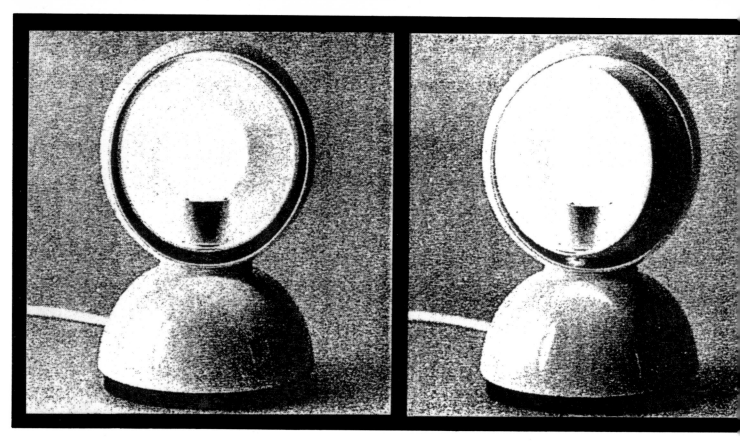

Above: Pictures of the Eclisse *lamp that show how the flow of light can be regulated by rotating the inner semi-sphere. Below, Studies for lamps.*

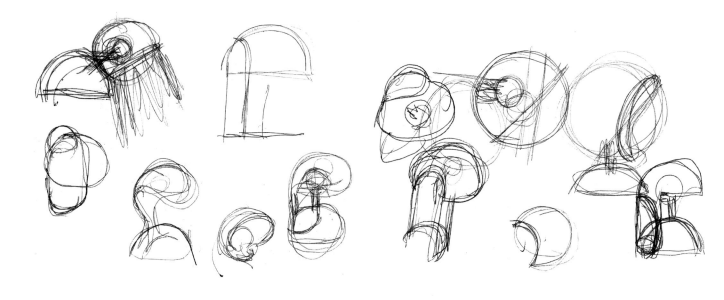

CONCEPTS AND DESIGNS

At this point we should begin to take a closer look at Magistretti's design method. Granted, the word "method" may seem inappropriate for a designer whose approach is essentially pragmatic; Magistretti, like most of his Italian colleagues, has tended to shun the systematic research typical of the Ulm school. In fact, in many interviews he has deliberately promoted an image as a designer who deals with each project in totally empirical terms, his solutions appearing to derive from conceptual intuitions that prove to fit the circumstances. He has even claimed that he can dictate a design over the phone. There is certainly much that is true in this; Magistretti's designs often seem inspired, an almost effortless arrival at appropriate solutions. Nevertheless, when carefully analyzed his output reveals a series of recurrent ele-

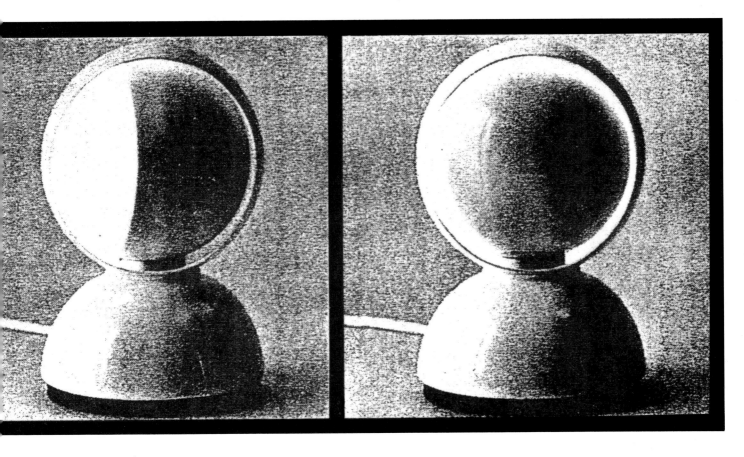

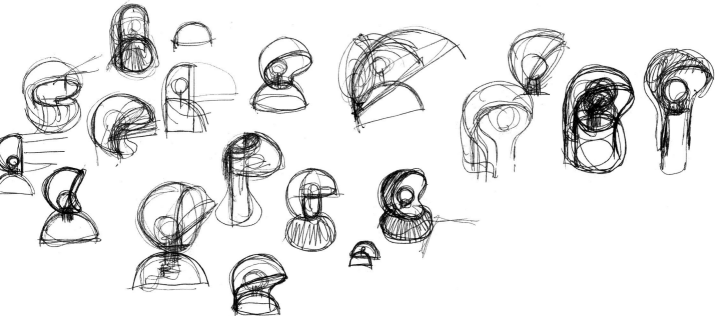

ments that derive from his cultural background. A closer look at a small number of objects will suffice to show how these elements are developed.

From the sixties on Magistretti started designing furniture in plastic. Two examples will be enough. The first concerns the *Demetrio* tables designed in 1966 using reinforced molded resins in what amounts to a revisitation of the stackable wooden tables Magistretti designed in 1949. "Among the first injection-molded tables of those years," writes Gillo Dorfles, "they constitute particularly meaningful examples of the way a new design process can be backed up by machinery to create essential elements of great formal purity."[1] Magistretti relates that he borrowed the idea from the photographers' plastic developing trays with

rounded corners made in Germany at the time: "I picked up one of the trays, I turned it over, and I cut away quite a lot of the sides so that I ended up with a little table that could be stacked on top of another one: so much for technological operations!"[2] As Magistretti points out, what is important is the idea from which the object derives — in this case sparked by observation of reality. It is also worth noting the self-effacement implicit in his reference to technology.

Later on, in 1969, Magistretti designed the *Selene* chair, injection-molded in one single piece of reinforced resin. With this item, however, he was not attempting to create a sculptural form that could also be sat on — along the lines of *Panton*, for example. His aim was simply to create a chair, a recognizable, familiar

piece of furniture. Two interesting plastic chairs designed in those years — by Marco Zanuso and Joe Colombo — have unscrewable legs, which are somewhat sturdy, in view of the weight they must support. Magistretti resolved the problem of the legs' strength differently. With the architect's grasp of statics, he opted for "S" shaped legs. (This solution is a development of an earlier idea, used for the legs of the plastic *Stadio* table of 1966. In the same year he applied the same principle to the *Chimera* floor lamp whose serpentine methacrylate structure is self-supporting.) The outcome is impeccable, both sound in its techniques and materials and sculpturally elegant, with its slim legs and uniformity. Typically, Magistretti attributes much of the success of the design to the ability of the technician who built the

model in the factory.[3] Other cases in point are the small plastic *Gaudí* and *Vicario* armchairs, both designed in 1970: the legs are the same, the arms have been created by cutting out a hole in the shell, and specific areas have been reinforced by thickening the material (in this sense recalling the sketch for a plastic chair made by Mies in 1946).

Magistretti has designed all sorts of furniture — for example, a number of famous armchairs — and even his "soft" items tend to marry a recognizable and sometimes even traditional look with the sort of technical innovation that can answer, or indeed give form to, the needs expressed by new types of behavior and ways of living. One of the best known of Magistretti's armchairs, the *Maralunga* of 1973, features a fairly normal basic shape with an

Magistretti with some of the Eclisse *lamp prototypes in a photograph taken in 1965. Studies for a lamp applied to a bed-head in an interior designed in 1964. A similar method for regulating the light was adopted later for the* Eclisse *lamp.*

innovative headrest that can be set in both a high and a low position on the back.[4] The innovation, however, is not overtly displayed but rather discreetly fitted into the overall design. The *Veranda* chair of 1983 is another example of furniture that can change its aspect. It has a seat that can act as a legrest, and a back that can become a headrest. Moreover, it also comes in a version with a rotating base that allows the armchairs to be placed in a curve so as to facilitate conversation. The *Sindbad* armchair of 1981, by contrast, effects change by adopting a casual, throwover cover, the original idea for which came from the classic English horse blanket. In so doing, the armchair both embraces and goes beyond the whole question of how fashion influences design, and vice-versa, a subject much discussed during

the eighties. The outcome is an object of remarkable, quiet elegance.

Another category of objects that has attracted Magistretti's attention over the years is that of lamps. An important example of his approach to lighting design can be seen in the *Atollo* lamp, published in the fiftieth anniversary calendar of the Museum of Modern Art, New York, as one of the most significant items in its collection. *Atollo,* first produced in 1977, and winner of the Compasso d'Oro award in 1979, is a table lamp in painted aluminum that owes much to the traditional abat-jour. Its simple shape consists of a spherical diffusor supported by a cylindrical element, which becomes conical in the upper portion. The diffusor actually seems to be almost separate from the base, to which

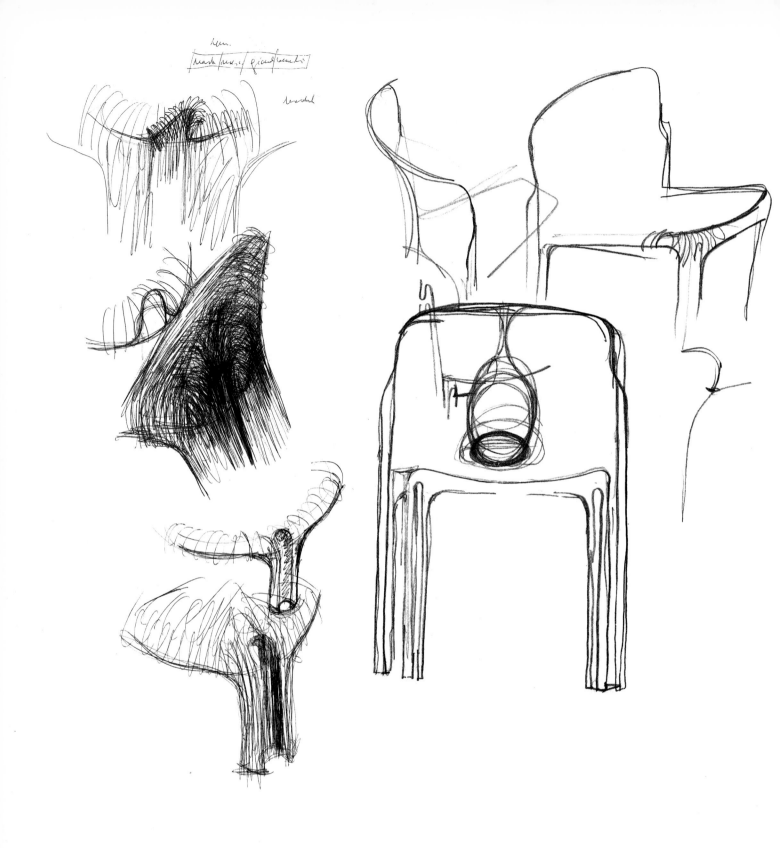

it is connected by a slim element, so that when the lamp is turned on the lighting unit as such appears to be suspended in midair. As with the classic abat-jour, the idea is to create a play of light. "It works well," says Magistretti, "because there are three different types of light: the black above, which the light doesn't reach, the bright whiteness inside the reflector, and the gray on the cylinder of the supporting element, which seems to be stroked by the light."[5]

Magistretti has often enjoyed creating plays of light in his lamp designs. The *Eclisse* of 1965 is another case in point: the flow of light can be regulated by simply twisting its two half-globes which share the same axis. The *Nemea* halogen lamp of 1979 revolutionizes the relationship between shade and base, the

horizontal plate reflecting light projected downward by a small porcelain cap.

The outer surfaces of the *Atollo* lamp are completely smooth and the geometrical shapes free of any superimposed elements, an achievement calling for a real tour de force on the part of the manufacturer, requiring a special unit to hold the bulb sockets and sustain the concealed diffusor.

We have dealt with this lamp in some depth because it clearly illustrates a number of recurrent features in Magistretti's work, some of which we have already mentioned. The lamp is the fruit of the combination of a conceptual proposal, expressed in several sketches, and the capacity of a given industry for translating this into real technical and productive terms. According to one of the

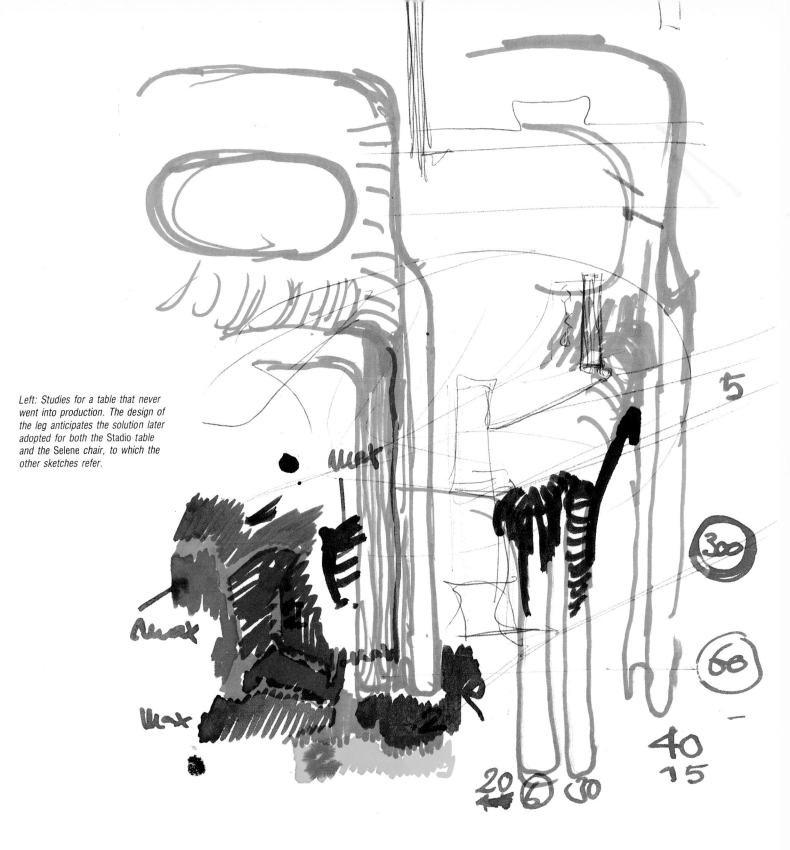

Left: Studies for a table that never went into production. The design of the leg anticipates the solution later adopted for both the Stadio *table and the* Selene *chair, to which the other sketches refer.*

factory directors, the ideas that Magistretti had jotted down "gave the lamp its form as such. . . . What took a long time and careful attention was the whole process of putting the design into production."[6]

"Design in Italy is born halfway between designers and manufacturers," says Magistretti. And rightly so, for the salient characteristic of Italian design is that it has the Italian furniture manufacturing industry behind it. As we have already seen, this is made up of small and mediumsized industries, which have usually been shaped by one dynamic, "Schumpterian" entrepreneur who identifies with the image of his firm and fashions it by insisting on quality products that are both appealing and culturally valid. Culture is a commodity that he is well able to use

for promotional purposes, and he occasionally also comes up with some design ideas himself. To this day Italian designers still work largely within such a setup, acting as consultants for marketing and art direction as well as purveyors of feasible designs. Such firms are generally too small to cover these roles with their own staff; moreover, the entrepreneurs who run them are generally too keen on their own views to act on the advice of anyone less than the cultivated, charismatic architect.

Another important factor is the special relationship usually established between the designer and the factory technicians. These latter often prove to be fully conversant with the most recent technical developments, and at the same time to have maintained the sense of quality and craftsmanship that characterized the best

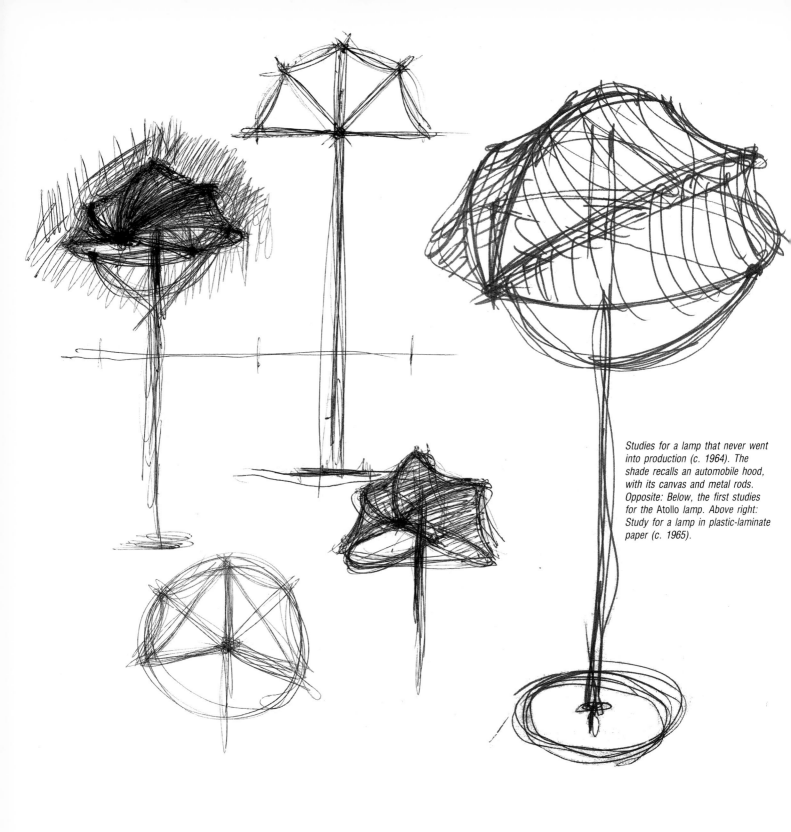

Studies for a lamp that never went into production (c. 1964). The shade recalls an automobile hood, with its canvas and metal rods. Opposite: Below, the first studies for the Atollo lamp. Above right: Study for a lamp in plastic-laminate paper (c. 1965).

carpentry and metal workshops of the prewar period, before the transformations of the fifties and sixties.

The design born from these conditions has never striven for the methodological and systematic unity that has characterized design in other countries, and in this sense Magistretti is a quintessential Italian designer. He puts it in a nutshell when he distinguishes between his own activity as an architect and his work as a designer: an architect must design everything, he says, whereas for a designer what counts is the idea, expressible in terms of a quick sketch. "The important thing is to know what you want, so that you can jot it down as a design, or communicate it by telephone. . . . In other countries designers submit extremely detailed drawings to the industries they are working for. But I don't do this, because it's not me that draws the pattern for the mold. I wouldn't know how to."[7]

Granted, Magistretti probably exaggerates a little in his fondness for self-deprecation. However, what he says is basically true, especially when added to the consideration that "to create good design it's important to collect up as much information as possible concerning materials, use, functions. Being a designer or an architect is not like being a painter: they're two quite different activities."[8] Magistretti thus advocates a conceptual control of technique in general rather than a real and complete knowledge of particular techniques. This approach to design can enter into close contact with the world of the factory and production; indeed, the mutual respect thus implied derives directly from the

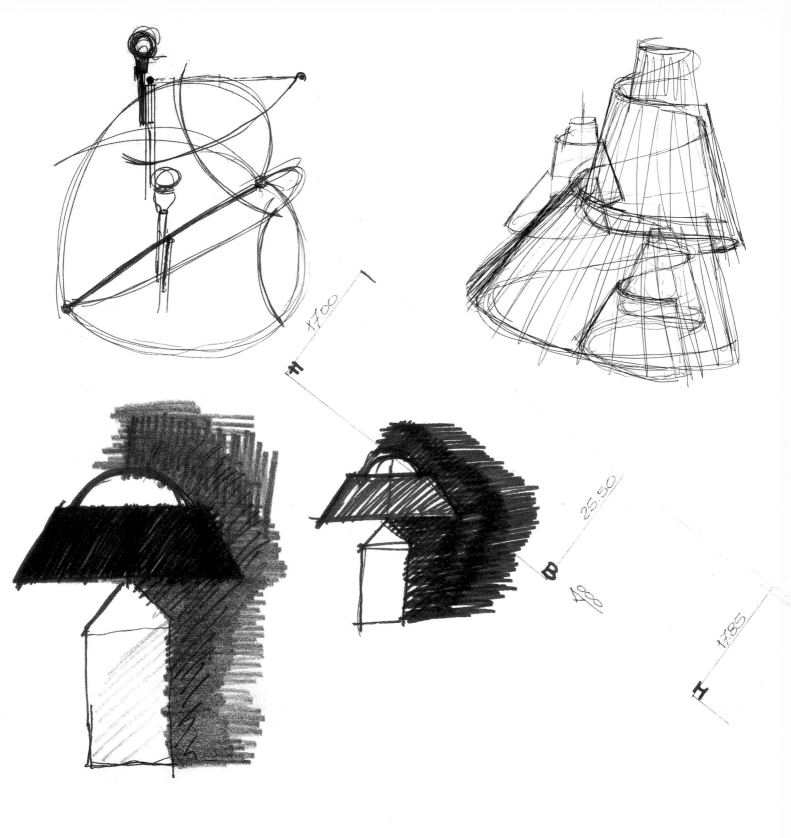

humanist tradition typical of Italian architectural culture as a whole.

We have described the technical complexity of the *Atollo* lamp, yet we are not able to see it in the finished object. The outcome is a system of forms, of volumes characterized by the play of light: the fruit of technical devices, but not an exaltation of technique for its own sake. The same can be said for all Magistretti's designs, from his lamps to his most technically complex items, such as the *Selene* chair. Technical content is used wisely and quietly, without ever making an overt feature of it.

Traditional objects sometimes serve as a formal anchor for Magistretti in his lamp designs, as is evident in the *Atollo* lamp, clearly derived from the classic abat-jour. On other occasions in-

spiration may arise from considering a particular object in a new light, or with a new use in mind. The *Eclisse* bedside light which owes much to the dark lantern, is a case in point. Both of these approaches are to be found in a number of Magistretti's designs, but the proposal of new types is most frequent in his lamps, possibly because they involve both new lighting technology and new materials, which respond to demands for new uses. Magistretti's lamp designs resolve and reconcile these various aspects by means of a formal structure made up of primary geometrical shapes,[9] from the semispherical, concentric caps of the *Mania* of 1963 to the composition of three semispheres in the *Eclisse*[10] or the two upside down cones of the *Pascal*, designed in 1979.[11]

Later, Magistretti took the process of simplification one step fur-

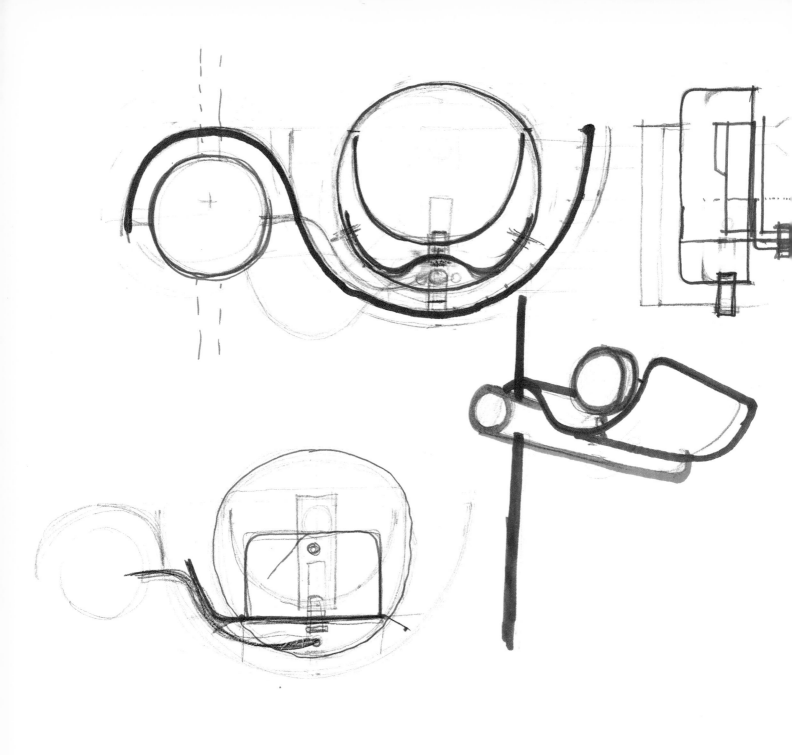

ther, moving in his designs from volumes to geometrical planes of almost graphic clarity. In the *Nemea* lamp of 1979, the circular base supports the small porcelain dome by means of a slim stem; in 1978's *Kuta* lamp, it is the vertical circle of the shade that becomes the main feature, with the stem a mere line and the base dome-shaped. The idea for this lamp probably derives from a Japanese fan.

The *Slalom* of 1985 recovers a concept partially explored by the Castiglioni brothers in their *Tubino* design of 1949, and develops it into an essentially graphic creation: a continuous line thickens at the base to form a stand and then develops upward to support a horizontal cylinder, which widens to contain the lighting unit as such. Looking at this lamp, it is easy to imagine the pencil lines that originally defined its shape on paper. Simplification of this sort — the search for lightness — was a feature of much of Magistretti's design work in the eighties, as witness the single curving line that supports the plastic shell of the *Simi* chair of 1984, or the 1983 *Veranda* armchair with its astonishingly graphic outline.

Magistretti's passion for pure geometrical forms can also be seen in the way he deals with details such as joints and hinges. Such elements are always reduced to their minimum terms, if not completely hidden; they are never imbued with expressive function. In the overall harmony of the geometrical composition, the joints are inessential, mere technical solutions to be handled one by one in the best way possible, without upsetting the general economy

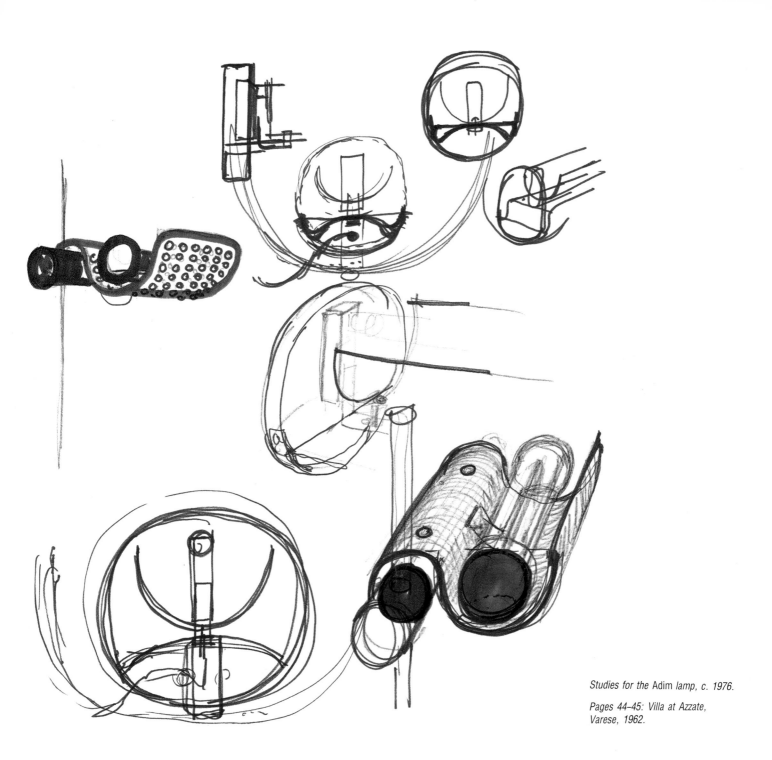

Studies for the Adim lamp, c. 1976.

Pages 44–45: Villa at Azzate, Varese, 1962.

of the outcome.[12]

In this sense the smooth sections, shapes, and juxtapositions of many of Magistretti's lamp designs speak quietly for the influence of a certain type of abstract sculpture. Of course, rationalist architecture has always shown an interest in abstract sculpture, and not only in Italy. A remarkable case in point was the Como group, and in particular the relationship that linked Mario Radice with Giuseppe Terragni and Cesare Cattaneo in the thirties. During the postwar period, in fact, a substantial part of Italian culture caught up in the momentum of the Modern Movement took a stand against realism. The sculptor Pietro Consagra bore witness to the event when in 1947 he wrote, "For us [Constantin] Brancusi's work is the most important in the field of

modern sculpture, because we feel that it points the way for our own future development." Design culture at the time was clearly moving in this direction, not only from the point of view of the designs themselves (certain of Gino Sarfatti's lamps are cases in point: the 1954 Compasso d'Oro prize winner *Modello 559,* for instance, with its two intersecting cylinders), but also thanks to the Compasso d'Oro, whose juries spoke out in favor of modern design and production. In the jury's report for 1954, for example, there was great insistence on "an aesthetic control that derives from a strict taste for formal simplicity and for figurative synthesis." This "taste" was said to be rooted in the "cultural reality that has grown up around the modern movements in the arts"; the objects selected as winners were those whose "essential

shapes respond to their individual functions." All this was to lead to "the essential simplicity that expressed the most cultivated modern taste."[13] At the *IX Triennale* in 1951 a special exhibition was organized under the title "La forma dell'utile" ("The Shape of the Useful"). Clearly both here and in the debate that ensued during the following years, the German concept of "Gute Form," as represented by Max Bill, was of considerable influence. For here too "the ideal to be pursued was the design of 'authentic' objects that suit their functions, that are long-lasting and pure of shape, temperate and eurhythmic."[14] Magistretti's lamps, with their smooth shapes and careful compositions, speak for an influence that initially derives from a rationalist background. They successfully combine luminous effect

and abstract geometrical forms, the former enhancing our perception of the latter.

There is no need to analyze more of Magistretti's designs to realize that all his work embodies certain characteristics.[15] He tends to treat each problem individually, and to come up with an idea that can be turned into an appropriate solution for the case in hand by means of a balanced formal composition. This then leads to a fully integrated collaboration with the manufacturing firm to perfect a prototype. The initial idea points the design in the right direction; but then, as L. Pareyson has explained, "The concept develops along with the development of the object, since this only really exists once it is finished."[16] To these points we should also add the rationalist basis that can be identified, albeit

quietly, in Magistretti's work.

Another aspect also calls for comment, however: critics commenting on Magistretti's designs — and the present author is no exception — are almost bound to have recourse to the word "elegance." In reference to the *Atollo* lamp Dorfles writes, "We see Magistretti work with compositions of elementary geometrical volumes in order to achieve shapes of great elegance. This lamp, despite the simplicity of the basic design concept, is so well proportioned that it assumes the characteristics of a major furnishing feature."[17] This introduces further elements for reflection: what does Magistretti's elegance really come down to? Part of it must be his design ability, his gift for geometrical control and appropriate proportion. This is related to his pursuit of for-

mal balance, the "classical" bent that is so clearly opposed to avant-garde trends. The critic P. Burger uses the term "organic" in this sense and not as current architectural criticism has used it: in his view "organic" is the opposite to both "disorganic" and "avant-garde," rather as Hegel opposed "classical" to "romantic." "In an organic work," writes Burger, "the constructive principle dominates all the parts and unites them; by contrast, the avant-garde work is characterized by far greater autonomy among the single parts with respect to the whole."[18]

But it is the concept of a "furnishing feature" that is likely to prove most helpful in understanding Magistretti's designs. With their great formal composure and their discreetly innovative aspects, these belong to a way of living that is a direct reflection

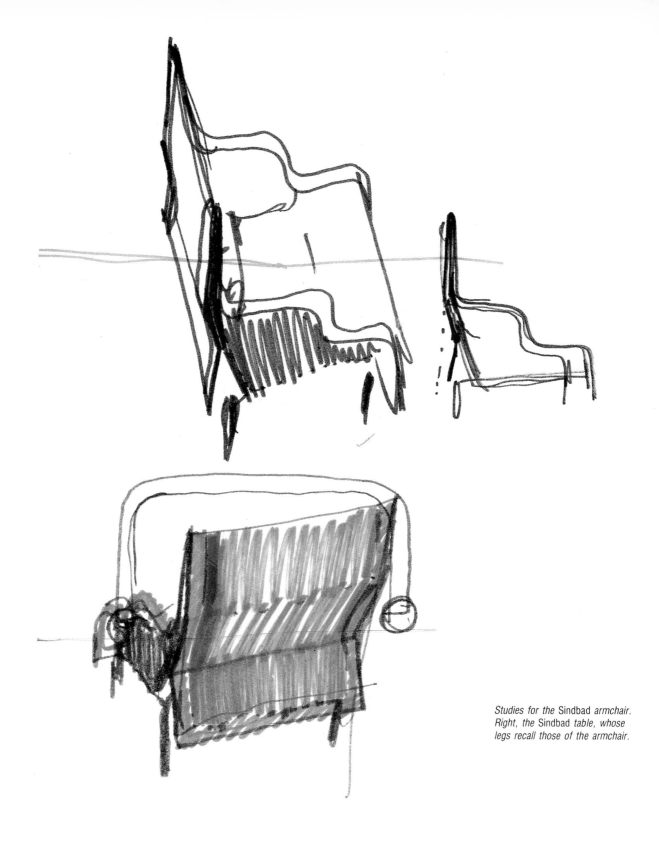

Studies for the Sindbad armchair. Right, the Sindbad table, whose legs recall those of the armchair.

of the designer himself. Magistretti is the first to admit that he only designs things he himself could use; indeed, his own homes have often featured his own designs. Thus the designer's life, his social and cultural world, all act as inspiration. And it is no coincidence that he is proud of his Milanese origins, of his architect great-great-grandfather (around the turn of the eighteenth century), great-grandfather, and father.

In a 1956 article on Magistretti, Vittorio Gregotti discusses "a line of Milanese architects stretching from Ignazio Gardella to Gigi Caccia Dominioni, all of whom share a taste for aristocratically reserved objects that are built with true inspiration and great craftsmanship, and seem to have always been there; objects that set the general tone and express a balance of values rather than dramatically draw attention to new shapes."[19] Gregotti identifies these architects by means of their shared taste. During the seventeenth century, the concept of taste implied the realm of social and civil ethics more than that of aesthetics. "Taste embraced the humanist ideal of 'sensibility' and 'culture,' as expressed by the man of parts, of tact. The man of tact is the gentleman, he who has 'good taste'."[20] David Hume and Lord Kames claimed in the eighteenth century that the standard of taste was founded on the universal consent of a particular class or culture. The Lodovico Barbiano di Belgiojosos, the Luigi Caccia Dominionis and the Vico Magistrettis of this world are intellectuals and architects who work with the Lombard bourgeoisie to promote industrial production within the perspective of an enlightened cultural tradition. Their ethical and aesthetic values favor sobriety and abhor ostentation and aggressive

shapes; they reject redundancy because it weakens communication; they are drawn by understatement because they mistrust overambitious interpretations; they court elegance as something natural and unaffected; they believe in mastering certain techniques so as to take part in an industrial culture that prefers to use technology rather than to exalt it; and they are open to innovation without turning their backs on tradition.

Such a social and civil morality not only makes adhesion to the Modern Movement seem natural, but also sharpens its ethical tension and formal rigour. This sort of restrained elegance and taste for natural simplicity recalls the work of certain designers working in France during the twenties and thirties: Pierre Chareau, Eileen Gray, Robert Mallet-Stevens, Michel Roux-Spitz. There are obvious differences, of course; most important

the attempt to shape "popular taste" as a "mediation between the avant-garde and tradition"[21] failed in France largely because there was no industrial and social development equivalent to what took place in Italy during the fifties and beyond. It was from those years that Magistretti started dealing with new problems in his designs: industrial and mass production, new techniques and new customs.

Magistretti's adherence to rationalism encouraged him to experiment with mass production in the most natural way possible; it is no coincidence that his activity as a designer hit its stride between the fifties and the sixties, when the furniture manufacturing industry was also undergoing considerable development. As he himself has declared, he is not interested in designing individual craft objects: what he aims at is achieving an intrinsically com-

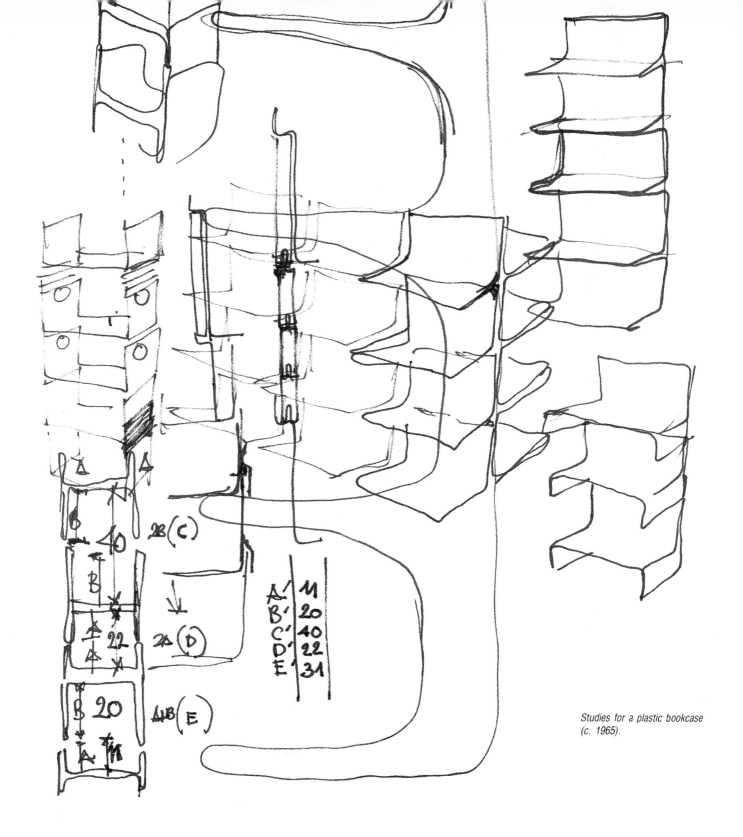

Studies for a plastic bookcase (c. 1965).

municative balance between modernity and tradition. This is very different from the pursuit of refined individuality that has characterized other sectors of Italian architecture since the thirties. Thus Magistretti stands out as one of the main exponents of that group of Italian designers who during the sixties paved the way for "a new culture of design for the home."[22]

Since then Magistretti's work has continued with extraordinary coherence. A glance at his designs of the late eighties — a period which saw the decline of the short-lived Italian neo-avant-garde movements, both postmodern and neomodern, their output reduced to arid questions of form for its own sake — makes this quite clear. During those same years Magistretti came up with a number of designs that deliberately derived from traditional objects: an inn chair, an English clubhouse armchair, even the *811*

chair designed in 1925 by Breuer for Thonet. In particular, a redesign of a traditional Venetian chair, the *Marocca,* carefully followed the same approach adopted nearly twenty-five years earlier for the *Carimate.*

All of these items bear Magistretti's hallmark of simplicity and elegance. In so doing, they begin a trend for more restrained furniture design in Italy, for objects that respect and reflect tradition and anonymous craftsmanship without being stifled by them. Granted, such products may not answer questions regarding future perspectives and directions in design. But then Magistretti has always preferred understatement to grandiose projects, small concrete facts to pompous theories. In its clarity and coherence, his work speaks for a way of life that has won him many admirers and disciples.

1. See Gillo Dorfles's comment on the Demetrio tables, published in G. Gramigna, 1950–1980: Repertorio (Milan, 1985), p. 237.

2. Giacomoni and Marcolli, Designer italiani, p. 187.

3. "I made it with the model-maker. If you look at it carefully," says Magistretti, "you'll see that it couldn't be drawn. To draw it I would have had to do at least one hundred sections. But there was this sublime model-maker, you just went to him and you spoke to him." Ibid.

4. "The Maralunga soon became the Trojan Horse with which Cassina managed to penetrate certain markets, especially abroad," declares Rodrigo Rodriguez, deputy president of Cassina. F. Bosoni and F. G. Confalonieri, Paesaggio del design italiano, 1972–1988 (Milan, 1988), p. 201. The same can be said for the Eclisse lamp, which, along with Richard Sapper's Tizio, has been a worldwide best-seller for Artemide, the firm that produces it.

5. Bosoni and Confalonieri, Paesaggio, p. 204. A solution in Plexiglas suggested by the manufacturer was immediately rejected, precisely because the designer did not want the light to shine through the cupola.

6. From an encounter between G. Bosoni and Massimiliano Mascherpa, managing director of Oluce. Ibid.

7. He then added: "In America good design is lacking because there is no contact between craftsmen and designers . . . . The Italian situation in which manufacturers and architects relate to each other is absolutely unique; it gives rise to the most beautiful objects without a design as such. The Americans design everything, even the owner's hairs. They come up with drawings that are perfectly useless." Giacomoni and Marcolli, Designer italiani, pp. 187, 189.

8. Ibid.

9. Dorfles points this out quite clearly when he talks about the "constant application of a design methodology that allows nothing superfluous and insists on compositions of primary forms that have been sectioned, pulled apart and put together again." Gramigna, Repertorio, p. 198.

10. In reference to the Eclisse lamp, Dorfles adds, "The Eclisse lamp, produced by Artemide, was awarded the Compasso d'Oro in 1967, and earned itself worldwide recognition and fame. It was commercially successful and popular to an extraordinary degree, and it was also admired for the formal qualities of the design and for the new image that it embodied: a lighting device, but also a neat-shaped object that was nicely proportioned and didn't take up too much room. Those proportions were the fruit of Magistretti's continual studies of pure geometrical forms and their possible modulations." Gramigna, Repertorio, p. 243.

It is worth quoting the jury's motivation in awarding the Compasso d'Oro to the Eclisse in 1967: "The commission believes that the object presented embodies the double quality of high aesthetic and design value and good commercial potential. Moreover, the technical solution adopted is innovative, in that the flow of light can be regulated by simply moving the rotating shade." Compasso d'Oro, 1954–1984 (Milan, 1985), p. 106.

11. Other examples are the toric crown of the Omega lamp which turns up again in the Erse, both of 1963. There is also the juxtaposition of spherical elements in the Giunone of 1969 and in the Lyndon of 1970, the simple cone and slim support of the Snow of 1973, and the cylindrically based Alega with its conic diffusor of 1978.

12. Here again we have the problem of the relationship between the idea of a design and its realization by means of production technique. What Magistretti has to say on the matter is particularly illuminating: "You don't know how to join up the two half-spheres that make up the Eclisse. The way the ring is made that holds them together doesn't affect the basic concept. Of course, if the manufacturer comes up with a great big thick ring that looks hideous, then you'd get him to have another go. But the important thing is that the lamp should open and close, to give you a small blade of light or a full beam." Giacomoni and Marcolli, Designer italiani, p. 188.

13. Compasso d'Oro, pp. 12–13.

14. E. Frateili, Continuità e trasformazione: Una storia del design italiano, 1928–1988 (Milan, 1989), p. 55.

15. Suffice it to add that, among the other types of objects not yet mentioned, there were also the kitchen lines that Magistretti started to design at the beginning of the eighties. Not surprisingly, his designs proved to be the first step in the direction of a return to traditional Italian kitchens after a long spate of American ones: a sensible sideboard rather than excessive rows of hanging cupboards.

In 1978 he also designed an extremely successful bed for a new company: the Nathalie was the first of a series of fully upholstered beds. The head derived from the Maralunga; a few years later the Ermellino was to have a changeable head and arms.

16. L. Pareyson, I problemi dell'estetica (Milan, 1966), p. 29.

17. See the comment by Gillo Dorfles in Gramigna, Repertorio, p. 451.

18. Burger adds, "The individual elements are devalued in so far as they constitute part of a meaningful whole; at the same time they are also revalued in that they act as relatively independent signs." P. Burger, "Avanguardia e engagement," Lettera Internazionale, no. 8 (Spring 1986). See also P. Burger, Zur Kritik der idealistischen Aesthetik (Frankfurt, 1983).

19. V. Gregotti, "Un centro ricreativo in Lombardia dell'architetto Vico Magistretti," Casabella-Continuità, no. 213 (1956).

20. M. Modica, Che cos'è l'estetica? (Rome, 1987), p. 35.

21. M. Tafuri, F. Dal Co, Architettura contemporanea (Milan, 1979), p. 229.

22. "With the brilliant quality of their inventions and their elegantly sculptural solutions, Magistretti, Gae Aulenti, Joe Colombo, Tobia Scarpa . . . and others produce what amounts to a new culture of design for the home. However different the individual objects and values, the fact remains that they are thus contributing to the most complete and significant chapter of Italian design during the sixties." V. Gregotti, Disegno del prodotto industriale, p. 280.

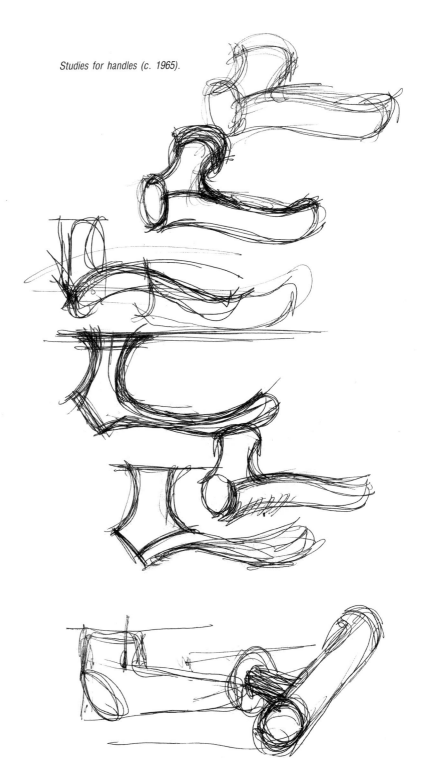

Studies for handles (c. 1965).

PASCA. Let's begin by talking about the eighties. You designed many objects during that decade. Which ones do you find most satisfactory, Mr Magistretti?

MAGISTRETTI. I think I came up with a number of interesting designs in the eighties. I worked a lot with Cassina, for instance, and I'm very fond of that armchair that hasn't sold well but has been copied worldwide, the *Sindbad*.

PASCA. Why the *Sindbad* in particular?

MAGISTRETTI. I'm fond of it because it's a horse blanket, not an easy chair. I was supposed to be designing an armchair, and this idea of the English horse blanket came into mind. It conjures up the history of Ascot, of the Derby, of the cavalry, with color and history melting into each other. And it occurred to me that it was so beautiful that I'd like to add four buttons and sit down on it. I like anonymous traditional objects.

PASCA. That's typical of Italian design.

MAGISTRETTI. Because these objects are extraordinary for the very fact that they are anonymous, and can go on repeating themselves in time with slight differences, because they're basically resistant to conceptual wear. An oar is an oar. It would be very difficult to design it any other way. They tried with the bicycle: the older models were more beautiful, but when you get down to it the concept has remained the same, even if they've now got lentiform wheels. I'm never interested in the stylistic aspect of the object, but in its conceptual content. I'm drawn by objects that speak for man's efforts at opposing nature, at overcoming gravity, at venturing into space. Why am I fascinated by certain Shaker objects? Because I like the idea of making clothes hangers on which chairs can also be hung, to leave the floor free. The fact that the pegs are made this way or that is quite beside the point. I remember that Gigi Caccia Dominioni gave me a lamp that he'd made with Livio Castiglioni when I got married. It consisted of a transformer, a camera tripod, and up at the top, a bulb taken from a sewing machine. It was a way of going back to anonymous objects and looking at them afresh, so that they can become something else. Quite the opposite to making an abat-jour with the tomb of the seventh light cavalryman as a base. That's been done too, and of course there's irony in it, but of a different sort. Anyway, I've always been attracted by this kind of re-use, not least because I don't like the design aspect to show too much.

PASCA. In the eighties you designed other objects that started out from furniture belonging to the anonymous tradition: the *Marocca* chair, for instance.

MAGISTRETTI. But I've always done this. One of the first things I designed was the *Carimate* chair. I'm anxious not to forget history, so I like to redesign excellent traditional models so that old species do not become entirely extinct. They need to be modified to suit our requirements, and then they can bring into the present memories that would otherwise be lost. It's rather like the way architecture tries to respect the existing environment, what was already there. This doesn't mean that we need to go creating ourselves a postmodern universe, like the Americans do. In fact, I wouldn't know how to set about designing postmodern things. I'm not master enough of the history of styles to behave like Venturi. Actually he designs intelligent things, though I don't like the

new wing of the National Gallery. Anyway, I like setting out from a concept in my designs, not least because this helps me to get rid of all stylistic preoccupations.
But to get back to the point, I designed the *Marocca* chair as part of a nice collection of furniture that I thought up for Maddalena De Padova, who's the most incredibly dynamic woman. I might say that working for her is not easy, at least not for me. It's a tremendous struggle because she's never content. But that's her magic. Actually it's a good thing because other manufacturers I work for tend to get all enthusiastic about something so that they're incapable of saying no. Anyway, the outcome of all this is a series of objects connected by a common thread, thanks to Maddalena. Give her a match, and she'll light the fire.

PASCA. During the eighties, much was said and written about what went by the name of "neodesign," with Memphis, Alchimia, and so on. These trends didn't interest you very much, did they?

MAGISTRETTI. No, not really. I didn't see the need for exploring other paths, for making a sudden break with a past that was and still is rich in inspiration. The past I'm talking about is the fruit of an encounter between classical culture on the one hand and the rationalist movement on the other. I'm certainly not able to decorate, but all the same I've been making recognizable objects for thirty years. So I've just never felt the urge to break away.

PASCA. You spoke earlier about the *Carimate* chair, which was originally designed not for manufacture but for a particular interior.

MAGISTRETTI. Yes. Toward 1959/60 I designed the Carimate clubhouse, and I needed a set of chairs. I remember that at the time I had a subscription to some northern European magazine, and I recall looking at all that delightful furniture of theirs. But it was also slightly boring, and I remember thinking: always the same things, very nice but . . . And so I designed this chair with its countrified look. I'm always happy when the objects I design seem to bear the mark of something from the past. I remember my grandfather's house, those courtyards, the spaces that I love so dearly and that, in some respects, are the opposite to the postulates of rationalism: terraced housing, the heliothermic axis, and so on. A fine Milanese courtyard can be so suggestive; if I can capture this, it seems to me to be much more important than respecting rationalist precepts.

PASCA. But in the end this chair was put into production.

MAGISTRETTI. Cesare Cassina came to see me, and he sat in the chair where you're sitting now and said, "Magistretti, how about us producing this chair?" And that's how our long tale of collaboration first got off the ground. He didn't speak much when he came here, and what little he did say was in Milanese. But I must say that I didn't get involved for a question of money. I clearly recall that in 1960 I had a bit of a nervous breakdown: I'd had to design a house, and that had just about done me in. And I remember thinking that by doing some product design I would be financing my golfing activities. I had no idea that in fact I was setting out on what was to become my main bread and butter.

PASCA. At the same time you also designed the Villa Arosio.

MAGISTRETTI. No, that was already finished by then. The 51

Studies for the Portovenere *armchair, 1989.*

22/8/89

52

polemics at the CIAM in 1958 regarded this very building. The house was at Arenzano, and had featured in "Casabella," meeting with Rogers's approval. The design also contains references to tradition, but not in stylistic terms. I wasn't referring to Italian art nouveau or to anything of this sort. I am basically a rationalist, but what's to stop me facing the building with slating? We were near Genoa, after all, and slate is a fine material that gets darker in time and acts as a good protective coating. And why shouldn't I use window blinds? I wasn't trying to create decorative effects; that's never been my line.

PASCA. You don't decorate, but you're no longer content with the ascetic language of rationalism. You need to relate it to the past, to particular places and their physical attributes. This is what was criticized at the CIAM.

MAGISTRETTI. Indeed, just as the Torre Velasca was criticized. The person I really owe a lot to is Rogers, who taught me to distinguish between what is important and what is less important. We're building within Italian cities, the most beautiful cities in the world. Do we really have to build with cubes in keeping with the heliothermic axis? Must the roof always be flat? Are blinds always useless? Blinds are useful, of course they are, they always are, everywhere. This is what's involved if you're not going to take things for granted.
I remember that Gigi Caccia Dominioni, whom I've always admired, was rejected in a competition once, before the war, because he was accused of using a sloping roof, and sloping roofs were not held to be modern in those days. Well, that's an old-fashioned concept of modernity. Our generation has come to the conclusion that being modern means holding onto the past with one hand, and onto the future with the other, and trying to get the two to meet. One of the reasons why I so admire classical studies is because they teach you to think for yourself, but also to respect what has been, to appreciate past effort no less than the efforts of the present. In some respects I began to understand this just after the war, when I came to work here in my father's studio.

PASCA. Was this your father's studio?

MAGISTRETTI. Yes, he used to sit here in this studio where I'm sitting now. He was an architect, and the studio was full of drawings. I remember it well: he used to sit at the drawing board and draw with a dip-pen. If I did that I'd get ink all over the place. But he was a magnificent draftsman. I'm certainly not; I can only sketch down ideas. However, I must admit that my sketches have a certain life to them.

PASCA. Shortly after the *Carimate* chair, you designed the *Eclisse* lamp.

MAGISTRETTI. I actually designed it, the concept of it, in 1966. The *Eclisse* was inspired by the idea of those dark lanterns that thieves use, the ones you see in films like *I Miserabili,* with a candle inside and a little door that you open and shut. Like the ones in the classic *Pinocchio* illustrations, where the thieves have white eyes and black clothes, and carry a dark lantern. Actually those miners' lanterns are the same sort of thing. I've always liked objects that can be manipulated to change what they do. Like the *Maralunga* chair.

PASCA. There's a great focus on geometries in the *Eclisse,* as in most of your lamps.

MAGISTRETTI. I love geometrical forms. I love making essential things that appear to be simple. In my work I find it terribly difficult to decide, and defining things once and for all is an absolute nightmare. If I had to choose a stylistically complex shape I think I'd go crazy. If I choose a cone, it's a cone. And I'm free of all those problems of style.

PASCA. How do you account for the phenomenal success of the *Maralunga* chair?

MAGISTRETTI. Well, I think that much of it is due to the fact that it's so soft looking, and to the magic of movement. People adore moving things, even if they practically never move them in reality.

PASCA. The *Selene* chair came just a few years after the *Carimate*. But the situation was completely different, in that you were dealing with a new technology.

MAGISTRETTI. You know, my use of technology has always been anomalous. I don't tackle it directly, in the sense that I don't draw the thicknesses precisely, or calculate the weights, or resistances, or whatever. So why did I use that technology? Because Gismondi of Artemide came back from Germany saying that he'd found this material that they use there for making photographers' developing trays and such like.

PASCA. That's typical of the history of Italian design, isn't it? Entrepreneurs who discover new materials abroad and have the foresight to imagine how they might be used in furniture manufacture . . .

MAGISTRETTI. A lot of those men were brilliant. My approach was to master the concept of molding. That's how I realized that you could take one of those photographers' trays and cut away one part, extend the edges, and so on, until you got a small table. After this I set to work on the subject of chairs. I didn't want to design a chair to be assembled using different parts; I wanted a chair in one piece, but not like the one designed by Joe Colombo, which was well made, had a strong image, but looked like an elephant. No, I want to design things that don't seem strange, that don't overdo the technology bit; quite the opposite to what the French are inclined to do, with their passion for futuristic objects. Futuristic is a word I loathe. The key to the *Selene* chair was the section of the leg. I think I dealt with the problem by using a particular technology in the most proper way possible, but without allowing myself to be conditioned by it, or even inspired by the idea of modernity for its own sake.

PASCA. What interests you most about technology?

MAGISTRETTI. I like technology because it's what allows mass production. Even at the very beginning of my career I was no good at designing Countess So-and-So's drawing-room, or Mr. Whatsit's diningroom chairs. This is perhaps what differentiates my generation from the previous one, from that of my father, and Mino Fiocchi, and the others, all of them refined Milanese architects who owed much to the Vienna school and to the Italian Novecento movement. They designed a great deal, but for individual clients. I've simply never been able to do this. Actually I did do something similar when I designed the *Cari-*

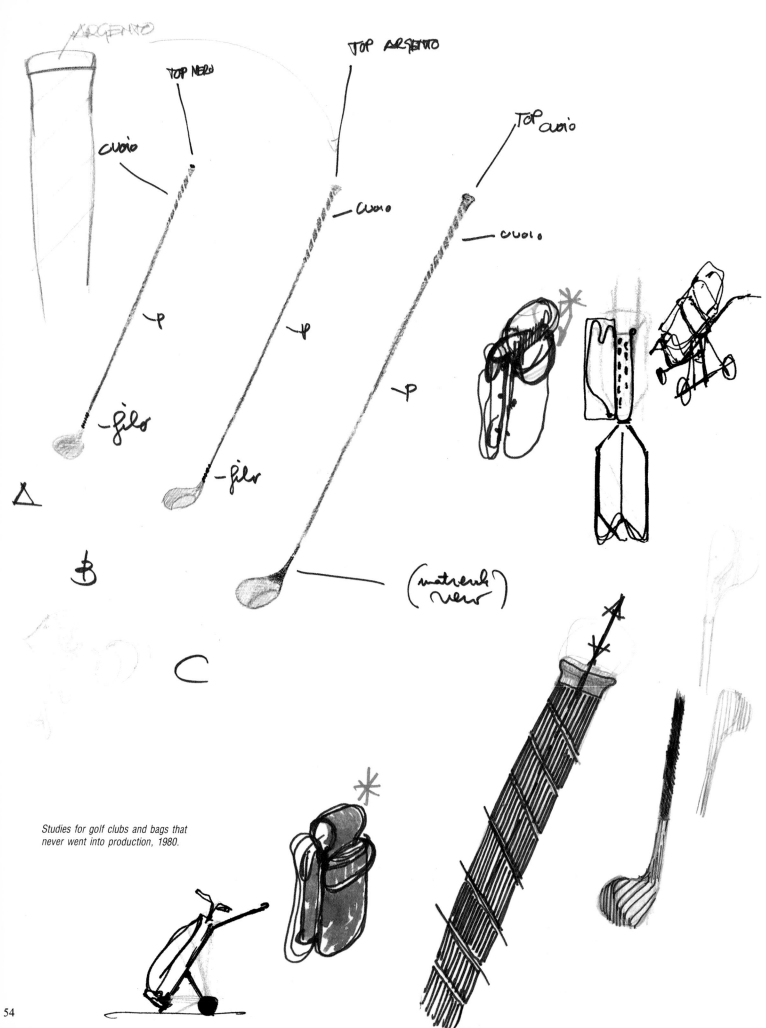

ARGENTO

cuoio

TOP NERO

TOP ARGENTO

cuoio

TOP cuoio

cuoio

cuoio

P

P

P

△

$

C

-filo

-filo

(materiali)
nero

*

*

*Studies for golf clubs and bags that
never went into production, 1980.*

mate chair, but then this went straight into production. It's probably my rationalist background that makes me interested in production on a large scale. Granted, some of my designs have been produced in very limited editions of maybe not more than fifteen. But my basic concept was repeatability, not uniqueness. So what I really like is teamwork, not with other architects, but with the people in the manufacturing firm. I need the sort of feedback that I get from production. For instance, only today I had a meeting with a manufacturer and his staff to discuss a project concerning garden furniture in plastic. I'm interested in designing these pieces in plastic, but I want the material to project a different sort of image, and to recall certain things belonging to my childhood. Now, this can only be achieved in close collaboration with the industry in question because these must be injection-molded objects that don't need to be painted, so that production is kept as simple as possible, etc.
To give you an idea, the uniformity of the surfaces could be a problem. I'm always asking Fiat: Why on earth make cars like shiny black Bechstein grand pianos, where you shudder at the thought of parking or driving through a narrow gateway in case you scratch them and then have to spend a fortune to get them patched up? In fact it's for this very reason that for the garden furniture I want to experiment with rough-surfaced materials. Today's industrial culture deals with large, if not very large, numbers. Collaboration seems logical to me.

PASCA. Do you consider this to be the real reason for the success of Italian design?

MAGISTRETTI. I'm absolutely convinced that this is the main reason. Today's meeting was a typical chapter of the history of Italian design. And while I was talking to these people I was also drawing, just as I used to all those years ago. It was the same sort of encounter with the same sort of industrialist and technicians. The only difference is that I'm now older and have more authority.

PASCA. This sort of a process could also have led to the designer's being drawn into the firm. Yet you have always preferred mutual autonomy. This is also quite unusual.

MAGISTRETTI. More than unusual, I reckon it's unique. I've never seen anything like it elsewhere. And I believe it really accounts for the fact that Italian design is still, despite it all, well ahead of the others.
One of the characteristics of Italian design is the role played by intellectuals who become so involved in contingent reality as to change it, and be changed by it. Now why didn't this happen earlier or more fully in other countries that were more developed industrially? Because the figure of the intellectual who gets involved and collaborates was missing. The contribution of the intellectual is considered indispensable. These gentlemen came to see me today because they believe that technology alone is insufficient. So they turn to someone who understands the concept of technology but knows nothing about company technique and technicalities. This is what gives rise to something new. The reason why the winning feature is the concept and not the technology is to be found in precisely this sort of relationship. Technology is a servant to be used with respect.

PASCA. Let's move on to another question. Do you use your own designs in your own home?

MAGISTRETTI. My place is full of objects that I designed myself.

They're autobiographical, that's why, like a diary or a little private world. I've created a landscape for myself, and this is where I live. My only theoretical support when I am designing is to think: Would I or wouldn't I have this in my own home? If I wouldn't, then I don't design it.

PASCA. Things are difficult today, in the sense that there's a lot of insecurity about what to do. A whole lot of myths, including the avant-garde movements of the eighties, have been swept away. And what remains is largely a feeling of muddle, especially for the younger generation.

MAGISTRETTI. I've been lucky really, in that I've had not so much certainty as clarity, and this has always been a great help. All things considered, I've always thought of myself as a product of the Modern Movement, of rationalism, even if I wasn't always very orthodox. In fact we were attacked at the CIAM back in 1958 for this very reason. As I see it, what's really lacking out there is any form of ideology. No wonder the world's a frightening place. You can't not believe in anything. Granted, we don't believe in that much either, but I do at least believe in my work. But the point is that if I design something, it costs me a real effort. Of course things are much easier for me now, but they still involve a lot of effort.
They say that design is in a crisis. Alright, so that may be the case. But in the meantime I carry on designing; I need to, it's my diary. For example I'm designing the interiors for my new apartment, and I've designed myself a sofa that implies a new way of sitting. This is the sort of concept I like. I've also designed myself other objects. It comes quite naturally to me; in fact it would be unnatural not to. Designing comes to me naturally, precisely because I don't believe that things stay still.

PASCA. How do you account for the success that your objects have always had?

MAGISTRETTI. One of the things I'm proud of is the fact that of the 120 or so objects I've designed, around 80 percent are still in production. I certainly don't spurn the commercial side of my work, because selling is a biological fact, it concerns the relationship between the object and history. We don't produce paintings, which are sold for little and then become worth billions. We have to sell, and quite fast, because otherwise our objects are dropped from the catalogue. Selling means understanding a particular cultural need, as it were, expressed by the general public. One of the great merits of Italian design is that it hasn't exactly created a style as such, but rather suggested lifestyles. We are lifestyle prompters.
What really fascinates me is the thought that in some small way I've influenced the life of a lot of people. Much more than I would have done as an architect. Because there are numerous reasons for buying a particular house, whereas someone who goes to a shop, sees the *Eclisse,* buys it and takes it home, in that moment becomes a creator. It's as though he made the *Eclisse.* The sort of design culture that we have here in Italy has spread well beyond our borders into all industrialized countries. We've given rise to masses of copies too, but what does it matter? It's the greatest compliment that we could hope to receive, because our limit, and our dream, is to design the archetype. In the end, if you asked what I should like to have designed, I'd reply: the umbrella, that extraordinary, technologically complex article that stops you from getting wet, that allows you to defy the Almighty, so much so that it was prohibited during the Middle Ages.

Studies for a house in Tokyo, 1986.

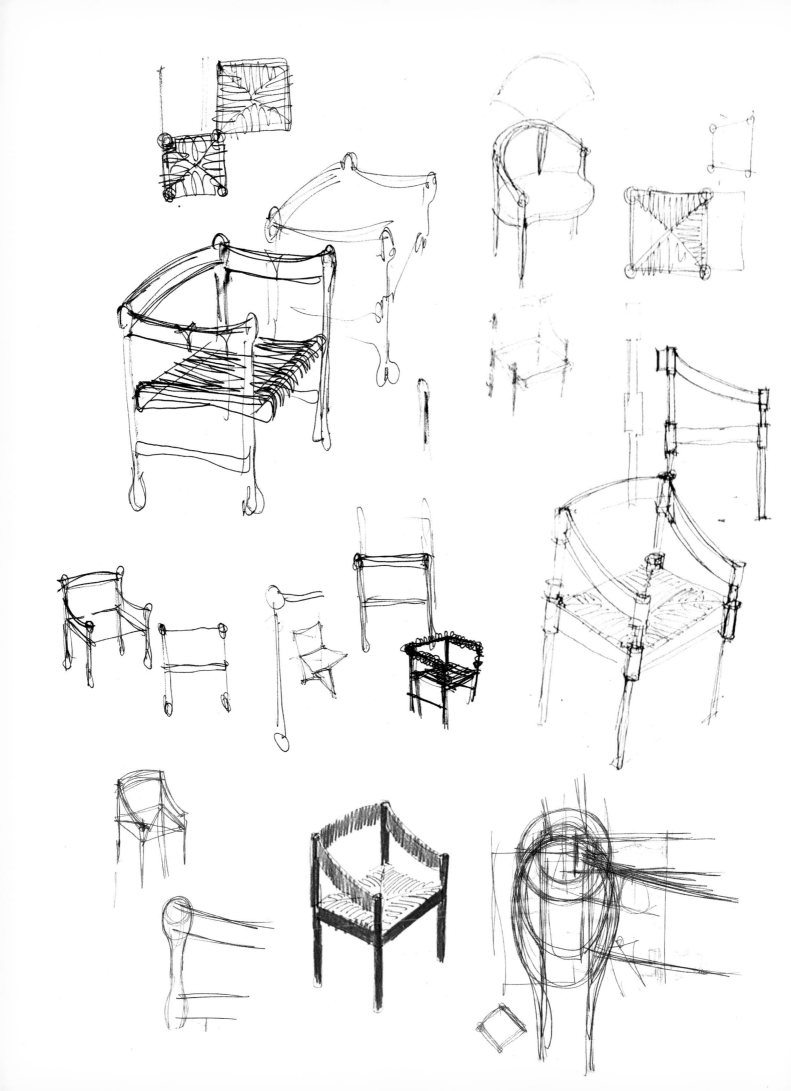

CARIMATE, 1960

In 1959 Magistretti designed the clubhouse for the Carimate Golf Club and this chair for the Club restaurant. It was later put into production by Cassina, the first chapter in a long-lasting collaboration.

The shape of the Carimate chair is based on that of the traditional country chair, made in natural materials like wood and straw. In this it also reflects the influence of Scandinavian design, well known in Italy at the time. The designer's attention focuses not so much on rationalist formal abstraction as on those widespread traditional objects whose functional simplicity frees them of stylistic influences and makes them suitable for modern homes. The red gloss paint finish nevertheless speaks for a desire to update the deliberate restraint of northern interiors, and indeed of Magistretti's own designs of the forties. Tradition is thus respected, but at a certain distance: Italian design of the period, this piece included, was looking toward the future.

MANIA, 1963

Although this is one of Magistretti's first lamps, it already speaks for his attention to balanced, essential compositions put together using sections of geometrical forms. This wall light comes in an opaline glass version, or in molded plastic. Produced by Artemide.

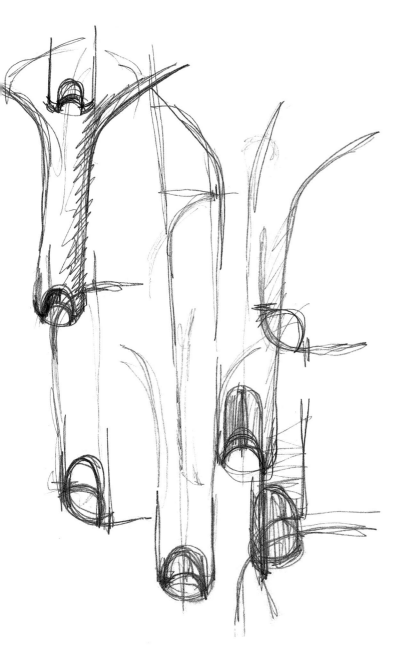

DEMETRIO, 1964

These items were among the first injection-molded furniture of the sixties. They are a development of the idea behind the stackable wooden tables designed in 1949. Simple and clean-cut, they are in reinforced injection-molded resin. Produced by Artemide.

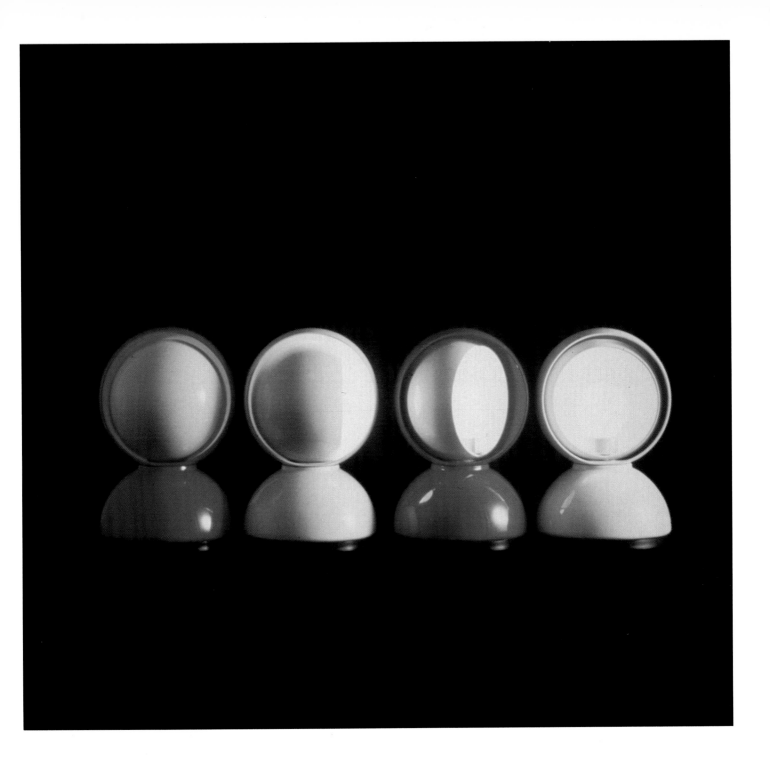

ECLISSE, 1965

Magistretti's designs often derive from an elementary basic concept: in this case, the designer realized the potential of a bedside light whose brightness could be regulated, rather like the traditional blind lantern. This small, essential object is made up of juxtaposed geometrical forms. Of the three half-spheres, one acts as a base, while another regulates the flow of light. As in many of Magistretti's lamp designs, the play of light accentuates the elegance of the geometrical shapes that make up the composition. The outcome speaks for his skill in designing simple, refined objects for the home that adapt to changing behavior patterns.
Produced by Artemide, this lamp has been extremely successful worldwide.

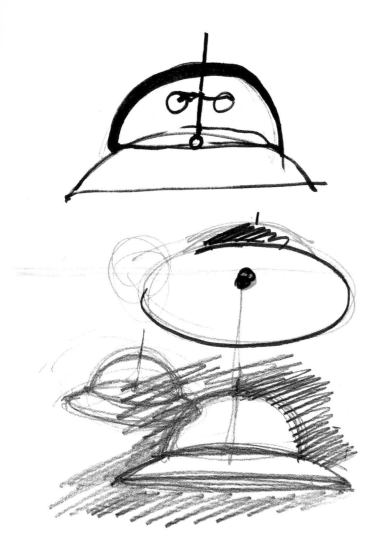

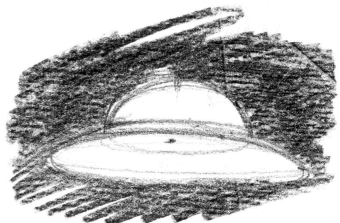

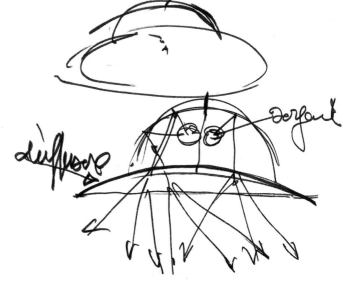

CIRENE, 1965

Floor lamp, also ideal for the garden, with a metal shaft that can be sunk into the ground and a hat-shaped diffusor that protects the bulb from the elements. Produced by Artemide.

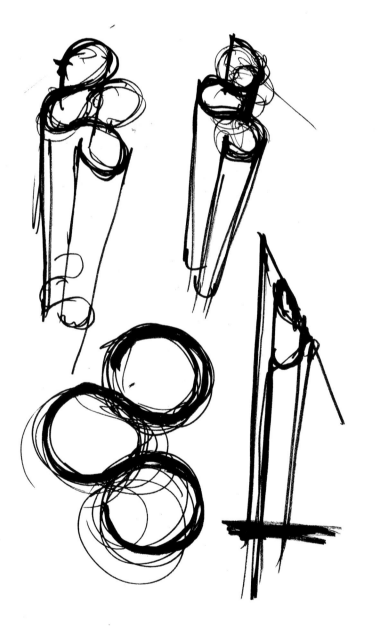

CHIMERA, 1966

This floor lamp is held up by the serpentine shape of the opaline methacrylate body. Produced by Artemide.

The main design feature of this modular ceiling or wall lamp is the luminous sphere of the bulb, whereas the poly-carbon support is extremely simple. There is also a three-bulb version (Triteti). Produced by Artemide.

66

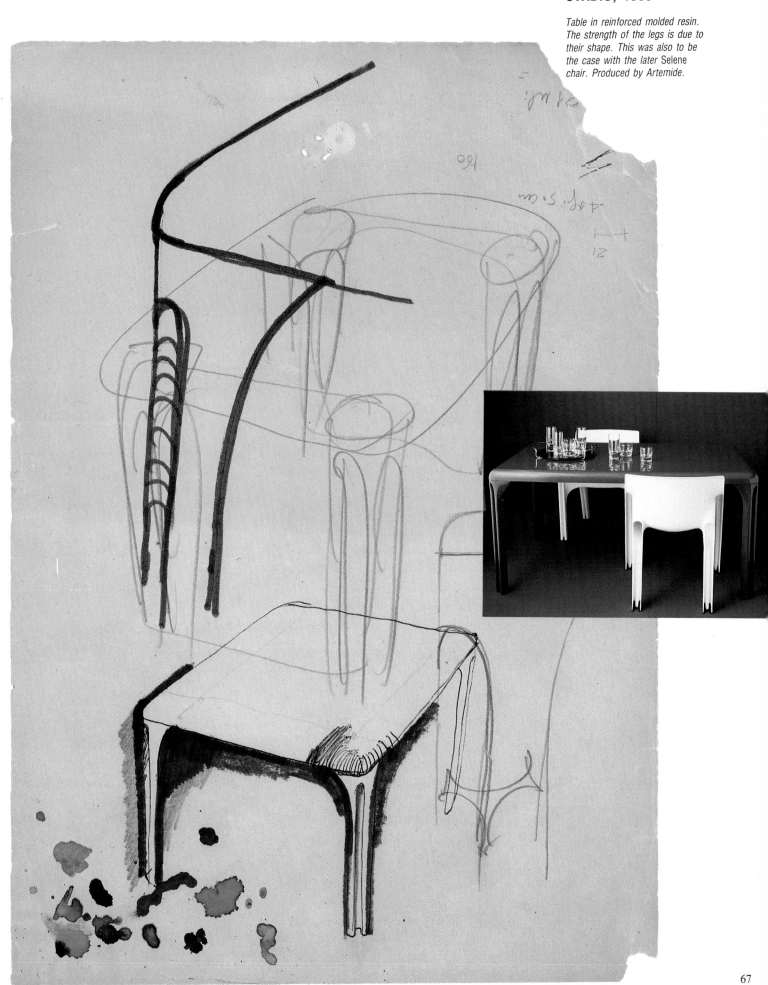

STADIO, 1966

Table in reinforced molded resin. The strength of the legs is due to their shape. This was also to be the case with the later Selene chair. Produced by Artemide.

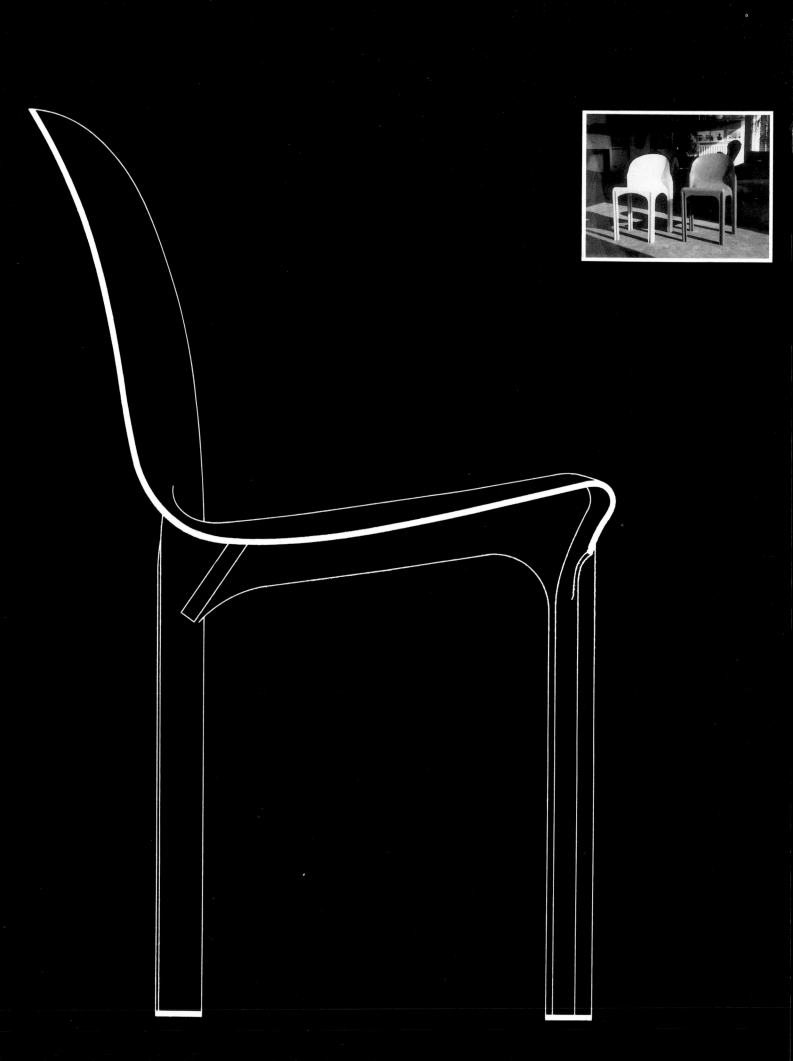

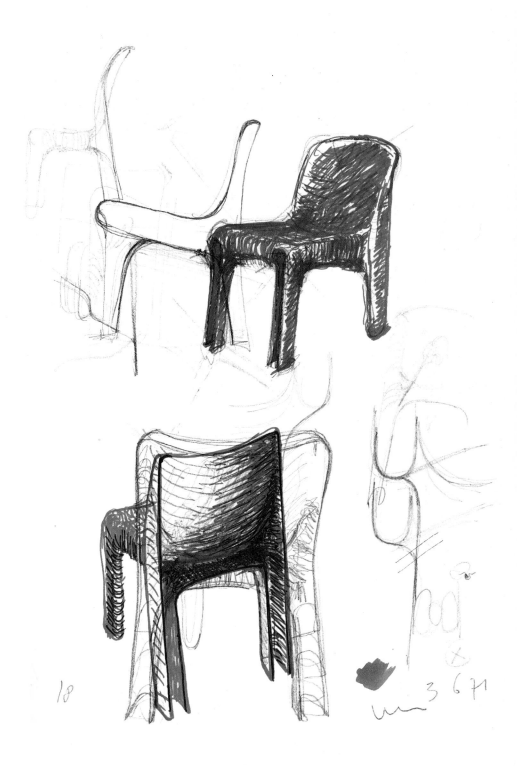

SELENE, 1969

Designed for Artemide using a plastic proposed by the company itself, this chair consolidated Magistretti's fame during the sixties. It manages to combine an appropriate use of new materials and techniques with a feeling of aesthetic restraint: Magistretti was not a designer to go overboard because he was using an unusual material.

The salient feature of the Selene chair is the way the legs have been achieved: their "S"-shape gives them strength that previous designers had found only in thickness. Moreover, this solution also meant that the whole chair could be injection-molded in one piece, which in turn made it stackable. The Selene has a quiet, recognizable personality despite — or indeed because of — the material used. Both the Eclisse lamp and the Selene chair have had a large role in promoting the world image of Italian modern design.

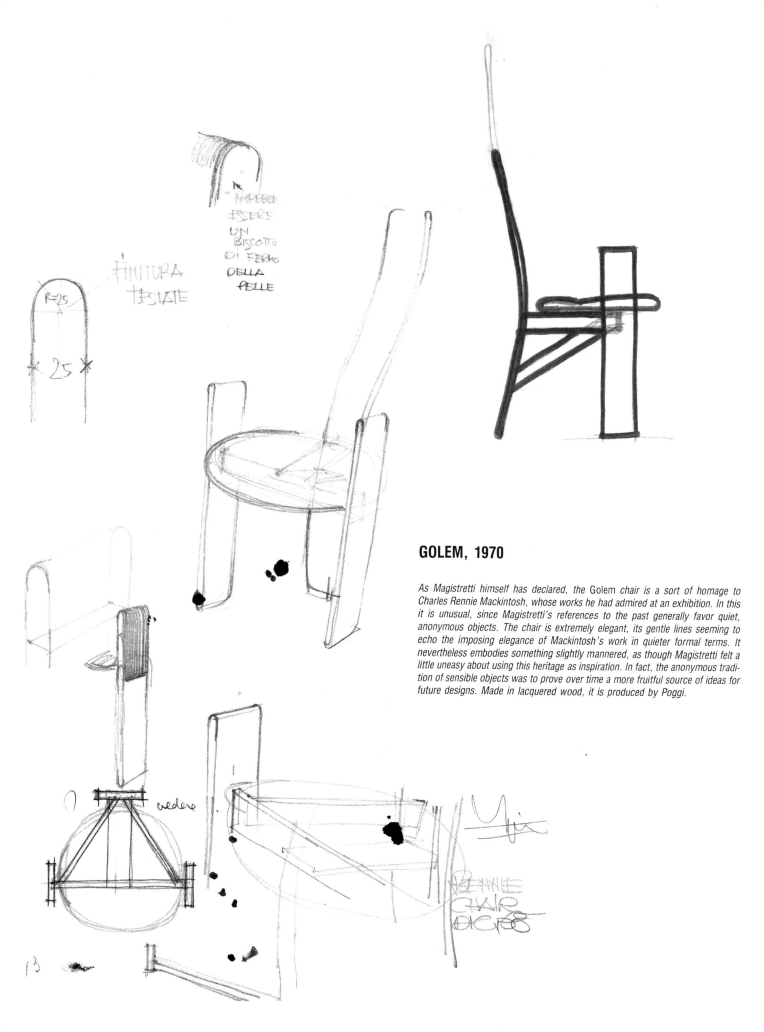

GOLEM, 1970

As Magistretti himself has declared, the Golem chair is a sort of homage to Charles Rennie Mackintosh, whose works he had admired at an exhibition. In this it is unusual, since Magistretti's references to the past generally favor quiet, anonymous objects. The chair is extremely elegant, its gentle lines seeming to echo the imposing elegance of Mackintosh's work in quieter formal terms. It nevertheless embodies something slightly mannered, as though Magistretti felt a little uneasy about using this heritage as inspiration. In fact, the anonymous tradition of sensible objects was to prove over time a more fruitful source of ideas for future designs. Made in lacquered wood, it is produced by Poggi.

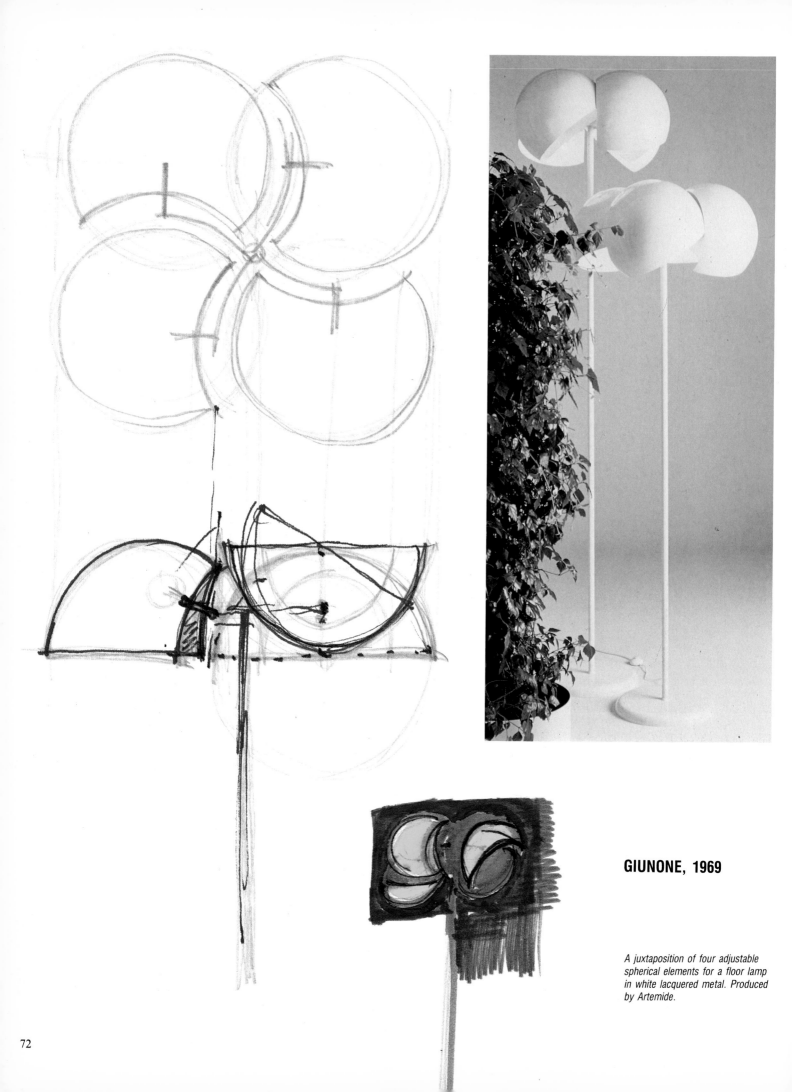

GIUNONE, 1969

A juxtaposition of four adjustable spherical elements for a floor lamp in white lacquered metal. Produced by Artemide.

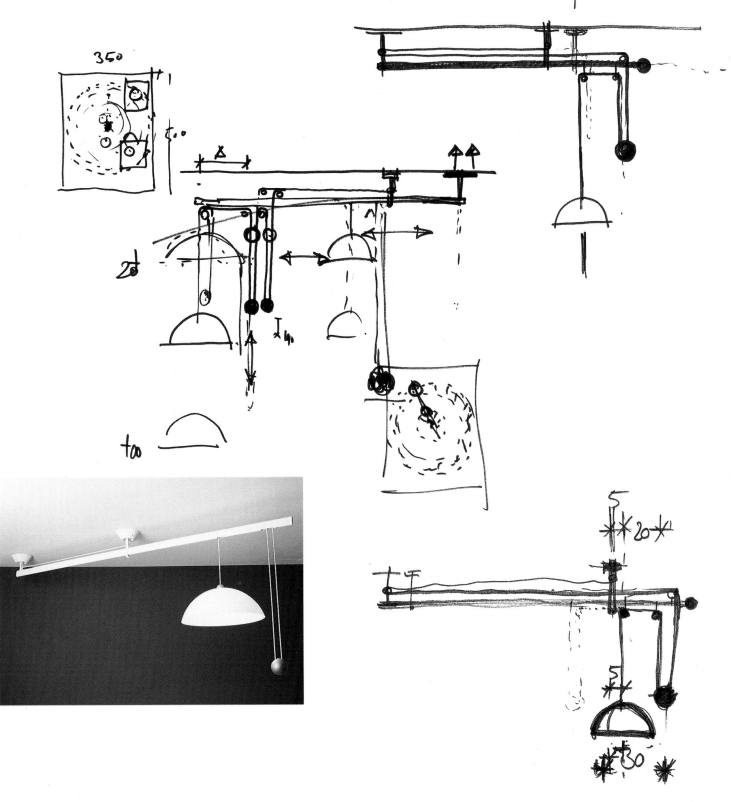

IMPICCATO, 1970

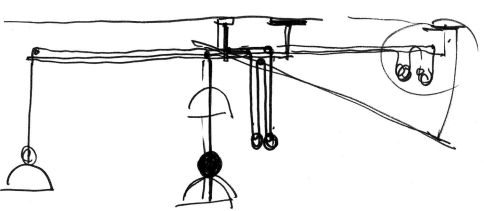

This ceiling lamp has a counter-weight that runs down a tubular aluminum shaft. This latter is fixed to the ceiling only at the center, so that the position of the lamp can be adjusted as required. Produced by Artemide.

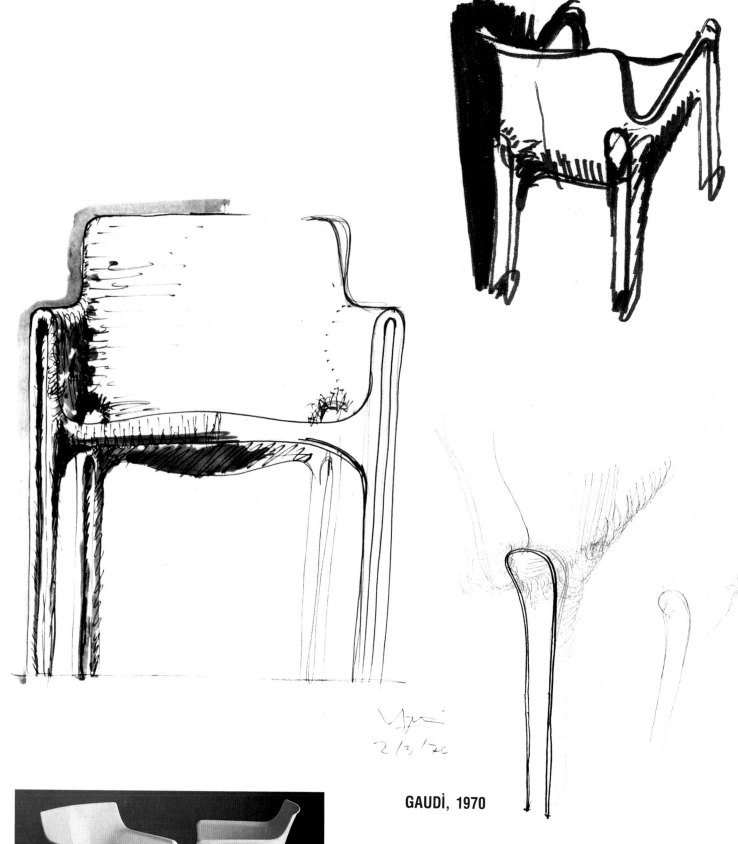

GAUDÌ, 1970

This armchair is a development of
the Selene solution, and is made of
reinforced molded resin. The arms
are an integral part of the shell,
whose inner corners have been
perforated to allow construction in
one single mold. Produced by
Artemide.

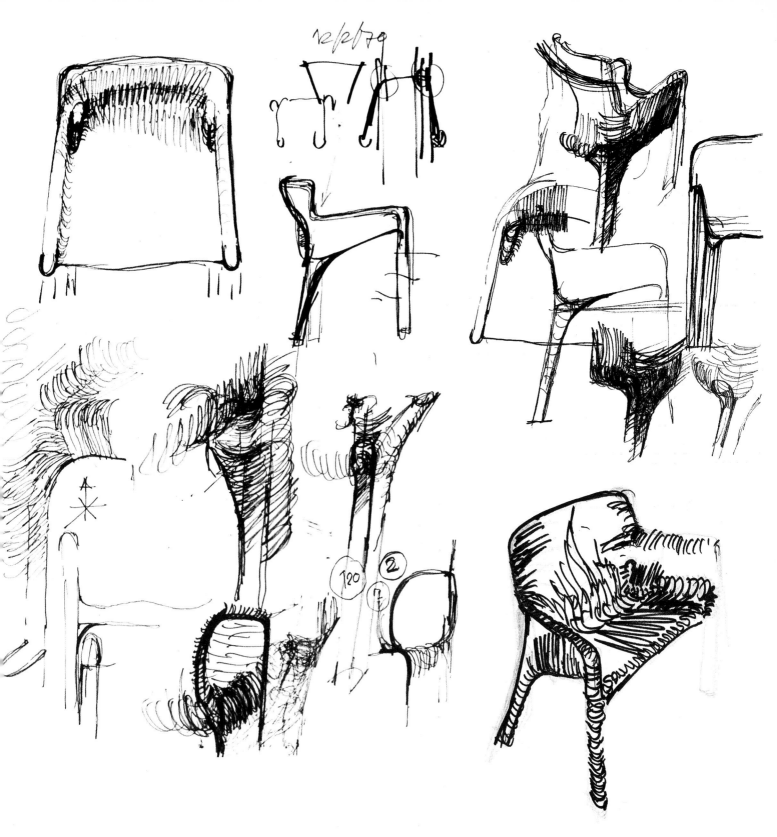

VICARIO, 1970

Like the Gaudì, this chair is in
injection-molded reinforced resin.
The sketches are studies of the
thicknesses necessary in the plastic
to support the various stresses and
weights. Produced by Artemide.

MARALUNGA, 1973

This armchair immediately enjoyed international success, thus helping Cassina, its manufacturer, establish itself in foreign markets and consolidating Magistretti's name as a designer of great versatility.

Magistretti's first armchair designs date back to the sixties, when he began using new materials like polyurethane. With the Maralunga, he managed to harness similar technologies to create a remarkably soft-looking chair, quietly innovative with its adjustable headrest. Nevertheless, the Maralunga is a distinctive design, one that was destined to be widely copied.

Magistretti's versatility was further confirmed toward the end of the seventies by the success of his kitchen designs (inspired by the Italian tradition of using dressers rather than myriad hanging-cupboards) and softly inviting upholstered beds.

SNOW, 1973

Floor lamp with a lacquered metal shaft. The diffusor echoes the trunk-shaped form of the base. Produced by Oluce.

PORSENNA, 1976

Table lamp in painted metal with fabric diffusor. Basic materials and a supporting structure of graphic simplicity. Produced by Artemide.

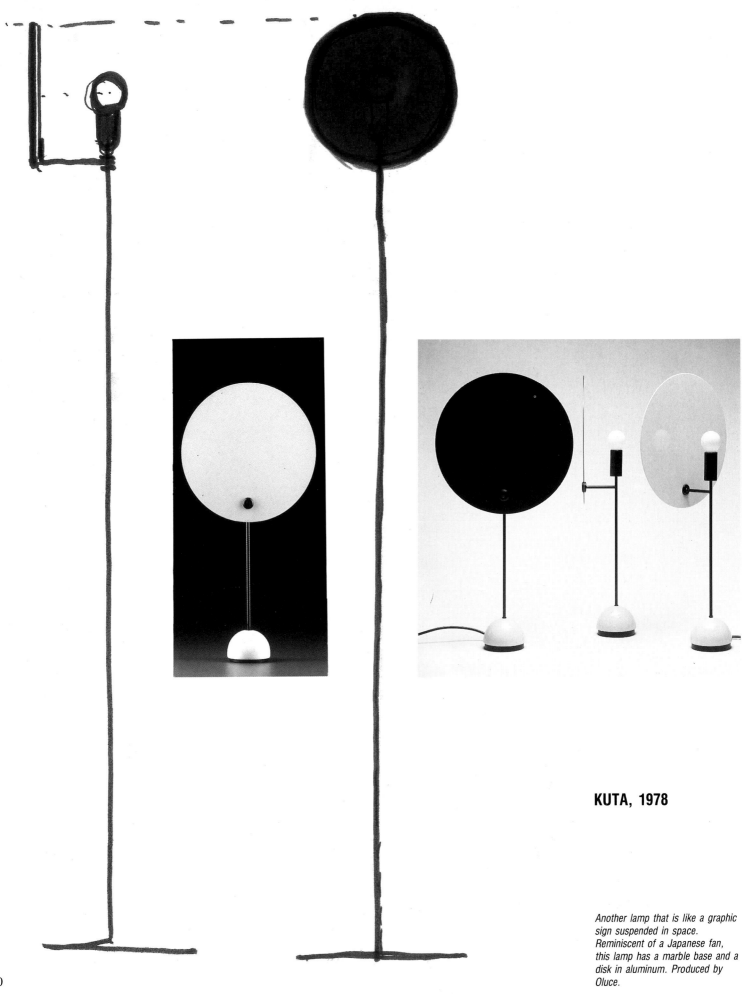

KUTA, 1978

Another lamp that is like a graphic sign suspended in space. Reminiscent of a Japanese fan, this lamp has a marble base and a disk in aluminum. Produced by Oluce.

80

NEMEA, 1979

The play of light characteristic of
Magistretti's lamp designs is here
achieved by the metal plate that
reflects the light beamed downward
by the small porcelain source.
Produced by Artemide.

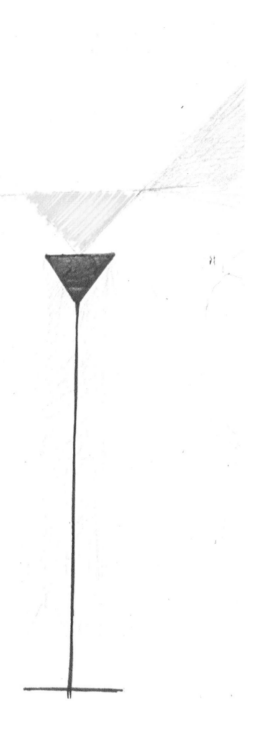

PASCAL, 1979

*This floor lamp is in lacquered
aluminum. The play of light derives
from the juxtaposition of the two
upturned cones: the cone above
illuminates the environment
directly, whereas the one below
does so by means of reflection.*

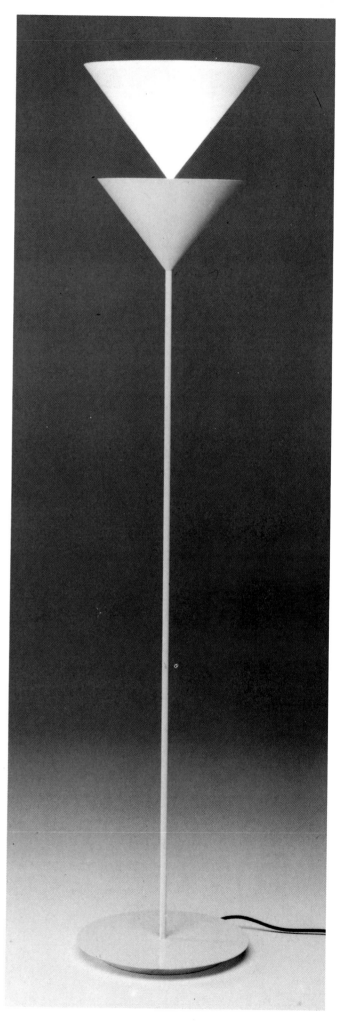

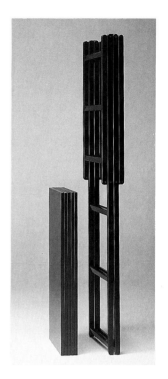

NUVOLA ROSSA, 1977

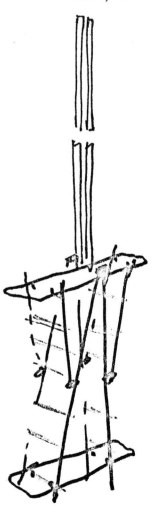

The outstanding feature of this folding bookcase is its great simplicity. Verticals have been eliminated and replaced by a form of bracing. Produced by Cassina in natural or stained bent beech.

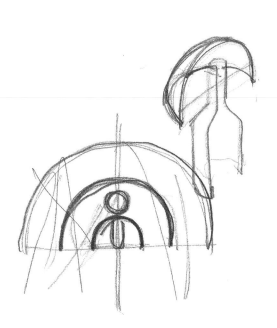

ATOLLO, 1977

The Atollo, perhaps Magistretti's most famous lamp, is certainly a clear example of his overall approach to design. A simple geometrical composition whose balance and proportion appear to translate the traditional abat-jour into a small abstract sculpture, it is made up of two main elements. The diffusor projects the light into the upper conic segment of the base, thus allowing a play of shadows to enliven the geometrical composition. Moreover, the diffusor is supported by an element so slim that it actually appears to be suspended in midair. These features together invest the object with an elegance both of material shapes and of the play of light. The outcome is a lamp of great restraint, and at the same time considerable personality. Made in lacquered metal, it is produced by Oluce.

From left: Tenorio *coat stand,*
Regina d'Africa *armchair,*
a study for the Tanganika *chair,*
Bath *bookcase.*

BROOMSTICK, 1979

This small series of objects, produced by Alias, is called ''Broomstick,'' a name suggested by George Nelson. At the time Magistretti was furnishing a small apartment supplied by the Royal College of Art in London, where he teaches. He was interested in designing foldable, knock-down furniture that could be easily transported. The basic concept was a wooden element of a given thickness, and at first glance these objects seem to hark back to certain almost do-it-yourself items of great simplicity designed in the forties. However, a closer look reveals a touch of irony: for instance, in the ample circle that enframes the sitter in the deliberately ''modest'' armchair; or the Bath bookcase, which derives from the typical English clotheshorse (a case of ''looking at usual things with unusual eyes,'' as the designer himself likes to put it).
This collection has drawn considerable attention but has not actually sold very well, possibly the effect of a mistaken image/price relationship established by the manufacturer.

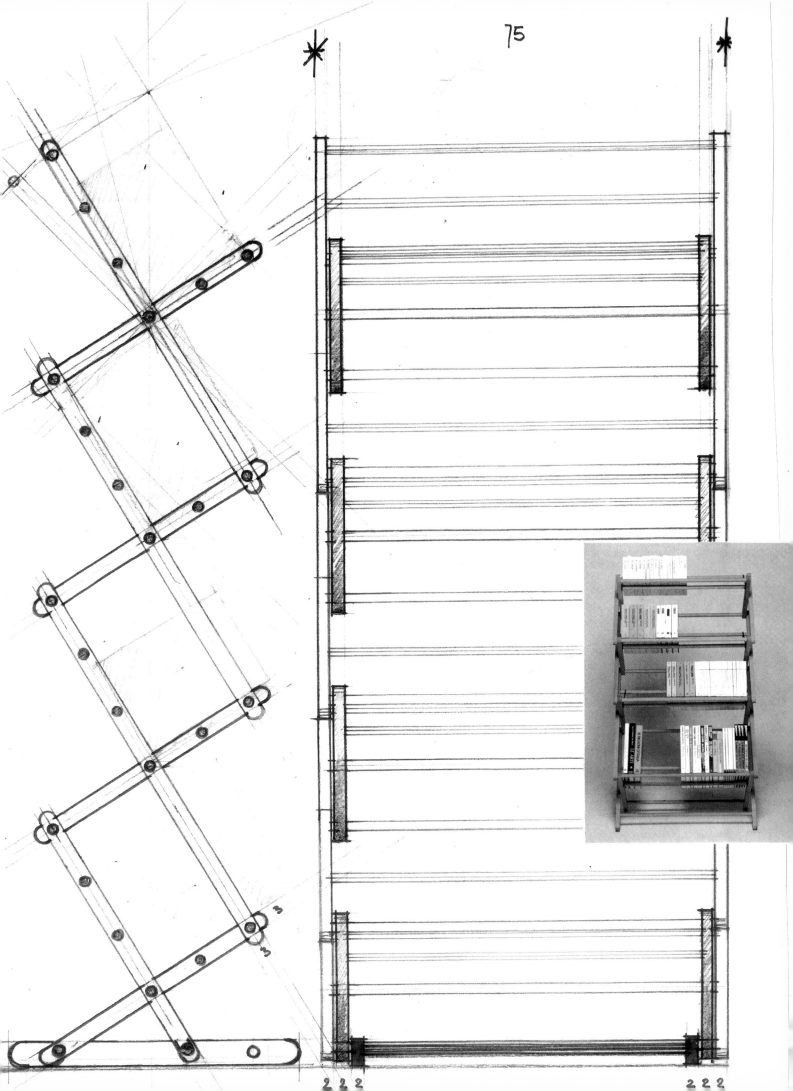

75

222   222

NATHALIE, 1978

This design speaks for Magistretti's great sensitivity to the market. It was produced by the new firm of Flou, and has been extremely successful. The bed, as well as the other items designed for the same firm that followed, appears to be entirely upholstered and invitingly soft, in that the hard frame has been deliberately hidden. This effect is heightened by the quilt and the cushions that adjust as backrests.

SINDBAD, 1981

Magistretti once had the idea of covering an upholstered armchair with something akin to an British horseblanket, and the Sindbad is the outcome. The bright colors and apparent simplicity give the piece a nonchalent air and a feeling of easygoing warmth. Self-irony and understatement are once more features of Magistretti's work: in this case, in a design concept that avoids all forms of excess and rhetoric in favor of quiet, amused restraint. Produced by Cassina, the frame is in steel dipped in polyurethane foam, and the base is of wood.

CUTLERY, 1980

Flatware of slightly self-conscious sculptural elegance, particularly in the case of the knives with their finger-rests. Designed for Cleto Munari and fashioned in silver by Rossi e Arcadi.

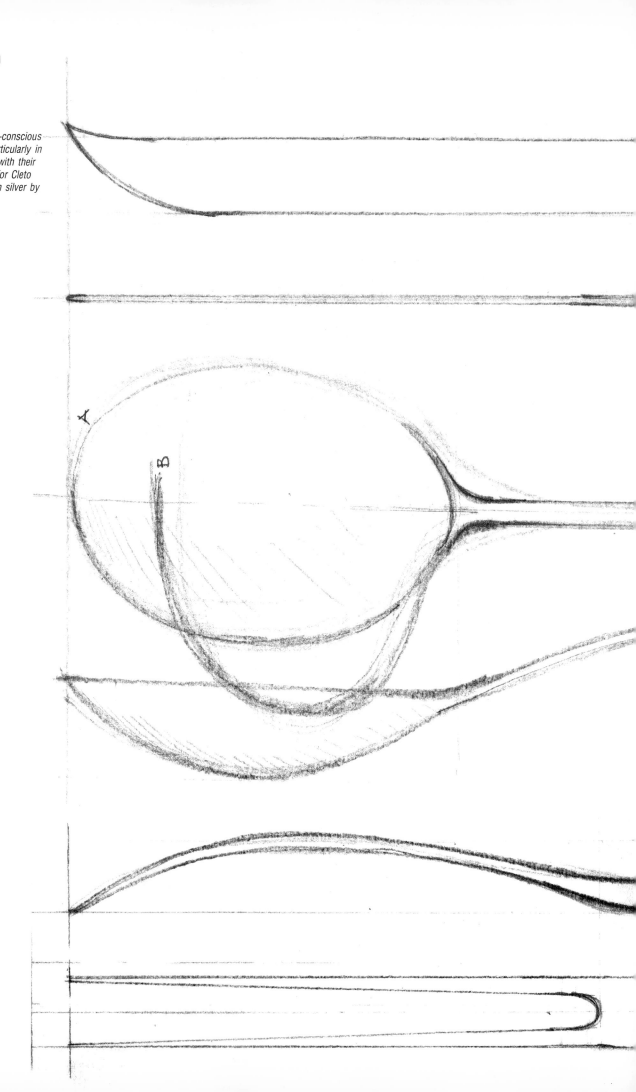

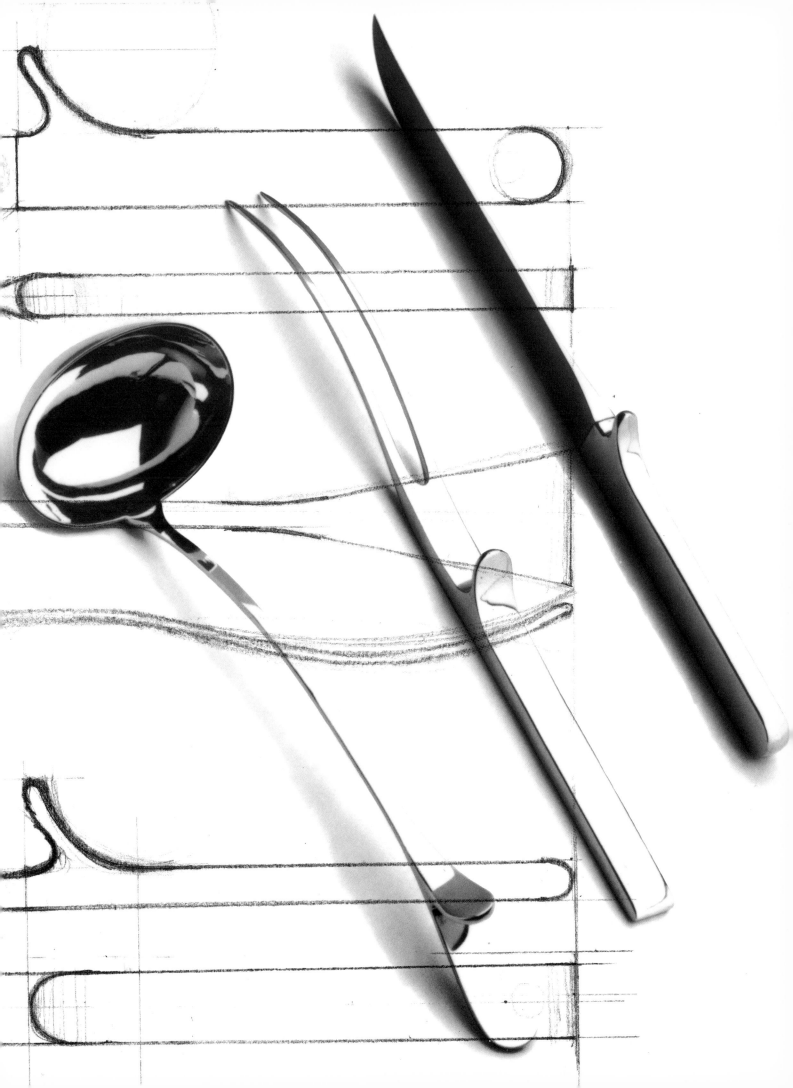

VERANDA, 1983

This armchair comes in various versions and belongs to a phase when Magistretti was simplifying his geometrical compositions to achieve lamps and chairs of almost graphic clarity. Veranda has a frame made of steel elements covered with polyurethane. Its elegant, supple-looking outline thus belies the strength that makes it transformable. While for the Maralunga chair this was achieved by means of the headrest, here much more can be adjusted: the headrest, the seat that can become a legrest, the various positions that the chair as a whole allows. Manufactured by Cassina.

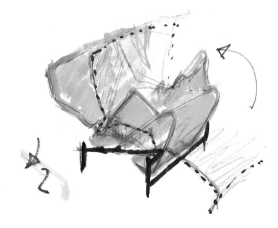

Veranda 3, *made in 1984, is a development of Veranda, and consists of a sofa made up of adjustable armchairs. The end chairs are fixed to a base so that they can swivel round to create a semicircular formation to facilitate conversation.*

SIMI, 1984

Another design of graphic simplicity that makes appropriate use of different materials. The seat is in polyurethane, whereas the base uses curved steel to assure the right degree of elasticity. The two parts are hinged together by a motorbike seat joint.

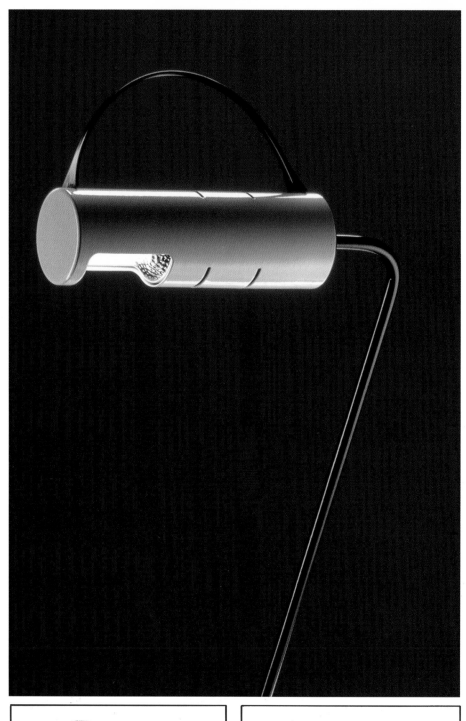

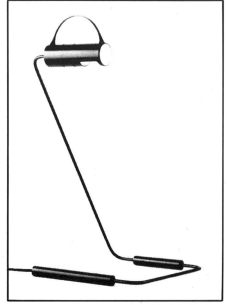
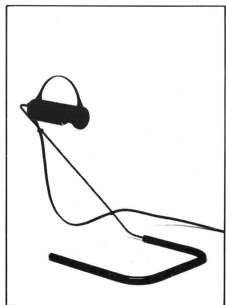

Again, a design that recalls a
continuous graphic sign. This metal
table lamp has a round shade by
means of which the flow of light
can be directed as required.
Produced by Oluce.

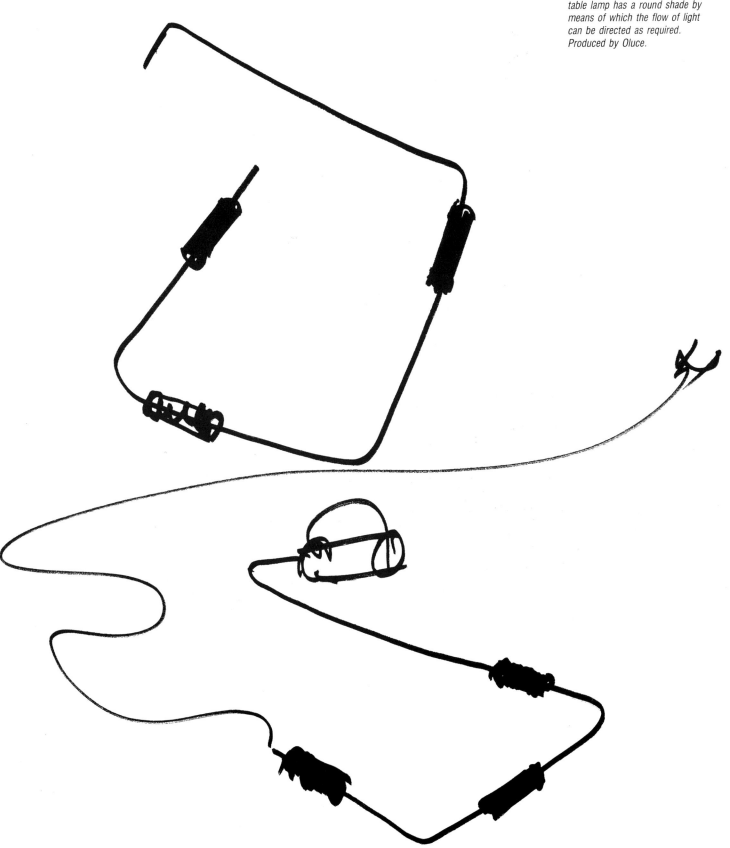

VIDUN, 1986

In Milanese, the name of this table means large screw. The adjustable height and the sturdy tripod base clearly derive from the traditional work table. As in the case of the Carimate, it is the use of bright colors that lends this item a contemporary touch. The base is of beech wood, and the top is of glass. Produced by De Padova.

SPIROS, 1987

This clothes-tree is like a tree branch that leans against the wall: the outcome is both functional and inventive. Made out of wood with a resistant painted finish. Produced by Morphos, Acerbis.

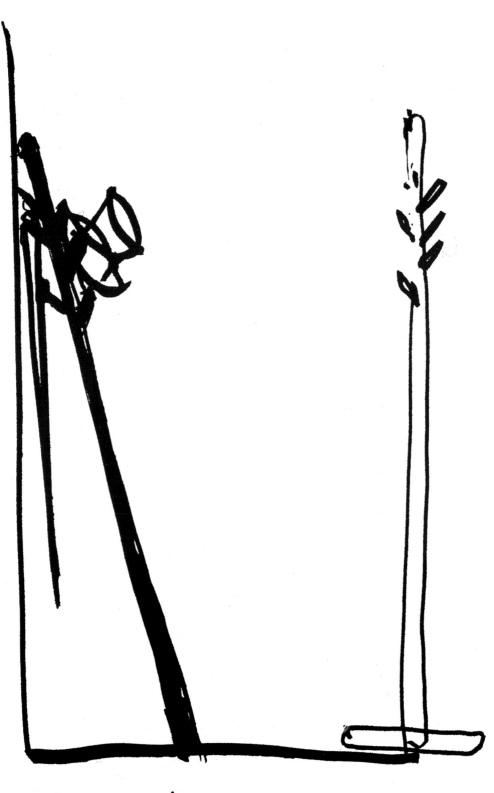

LESTER, 1987

Office lamp in painted aluminum. A special balancing mechanism inside the arm of the lamp keeps the reflector in a horizontal position. Produced by Oluce.

MAROCCA, 1987

During the late eighties Magistretti gradually designed for De Padova a series of objects that began to make up a collection. These included the Marocca, a redesign of a typical Venetian inn chair dating back to the eighteenth century. In so doing, the designer continued an approach begun with the Carimate chair, taking a new look at anonymous traditional objects to achieve elegant proportions and fine lines that could speak for themselves in thoroughly contemporary terms. Many of the objects designed by Magistretti for De Padova look back to tradition. However, while at first his interest in such a heritage was a way of avoiding the excesses of formal abstraction typical of rationalism, in time he probably also found it a reaffirmation of the ''authentic,'' as opposed to the gratuitous novelty of neomodern design.

SPIGO, 1987

This collection comprises a chest of drawers, a chest, and a bedside table, all called intorno al letto. *The small drawers can be pulled right out so that they can be used as trays. In American cherry. Produced by Flou.*

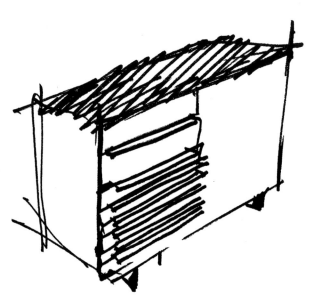

SILVER, 1989

This chair was also designed for the De Padova collection: it is a redesign of the 811 wooden chair designed by Breuer for Thonet in 1925. In Magistretti's version, the chair is made of electro-soldered aluminum tubing, with seat and armrests in polypropylene to allow mass production. Designed for both home and office environments, the Silver chair speaks for Magistretti's interest in the narrowing of the gap between home and office that has come with the spread of computerization.

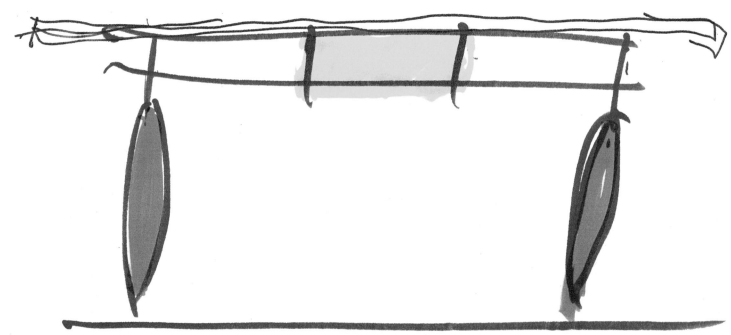

CAMPIGLIA, 1990

This is one of the series of kitchen furnishings designed by Magistretti from the seventies on. It is in beech, with frosted glass doors. Instead of the usual vertical arrangements, this line favors traditional items of Italian kitchen furniture such as the sideboard. Produced by Schiffini.

Department of Biology, Università Statale, Milan, 1978.

ARCHITECTURAL WORKS	**1949**	INA Casa subsidized housing, Piacenza

1950
INA Casa, Morbegno
INA Casa, Chiavenna
House in corso di Porta Ticinese, Milan

1951
INA Casa, Somma Lombardo
INA Casa, Lissone
Pharmacological laboratory, corso di Porta Ticinese, Milan

1952
House in via S. Marta, Milan
House in via Varese, Milan

1953

Credito Varesino bank, Caronno Pertusella
Credito Varesino bank, Olgiate Olona
House in corso di Porta Romana 113, with garages, Milan
House for Cartiera Fagioli employees, Rozzano, Milan
Cementi Rossi Laboratories, Piacenza
• QT8 district church, Milan (with M. Tedeschi)
Villa Majno maisonette extension, Milan

1954
House in via Cavour, Piacenza
Roma Hotel, Piacenza
Credito Varesino bank, Solbiate Arno

1955
Credito Varesino bank, Laveno

1956
Park Tower, via Revere, Milan (with F. Longoni)
Recreation center and cinema at Rescaldina
Office block in corso Europa, Milan
INA Casa, S. Zeno sul Naviglio

1957
INA Casa, Sedriano

1958
• S. Gregorio house and cinema, Milan
Credito Varesino bank safe deposit box room, Milan
INA Casa, Odolo
INA Casa, Concesio

1959
Rosenberg Bank, Milan
Arosio House, Arenzano
Lot 2 House, Arenzano
Lot 3 House, Arenzano
Lot 15 House, Arenzano
INA Casa, Pozzuolo Martesana, Como, Cinisello Balsamo

1960
Clubhouse and pool, Carimate Golf Club (with G. Veneziani)

1961
House, Monteolimpino, Como
House in via Leopardi, Milan (with G. Veneziani)

1962
House at Azzate, Varese
• House at Ello, Como
House at Arzachena, Sassari
House at Carimate, Como

1963
House and Tower, piazzale Aquileia, Milan
Houses at Roccolo, Pineta di Arenzano
Hotel at Campana, Argentina
House at Ghiffa, Novara
House in the Cantalupa district, Milan

1964
MBM Canteen, Trezzano sul Naviglio, Milan
Coca Cola Factory, Florence
MBM prefabricated buildings, Olmi District, Baggio, Milan
House at Arenzano
Houses at Framura

1965
Marina Grande residential complex, Arenzano
MBM prefabricated buildings and tower, Gallaratese District, Milan
Marina Grande apartment house, Arenzano
• House in via S. Marco, Milan
Cassina House, Carimate, Como
MBM prefabricated buildings, viale Suzzani district, Milan
MBM prefabricated buildings, Bovisasca district, Milan

1966
House in via Conservatorio 22, Milan

1967
MBM office block, Trezzano sul Naviglio, Milan
Cerruti showroom, Paris
House in corso di Porta Romana 53, Milan
House in via Solari 9, Milan
Milano S. Felice residential district (with L. Caccia Dominioni)

1968
Via Forze Armate district, Milan (with L. Caccia Dominioni)

1969
Church at Ravello, Rescaldina
• Cusano Milanino Town Hall
Primary School, Meda (with Gae Aulenti)
House in Trieste

1970

Houses at Arizzano, Intra
● Furnished apartment building in via Cesari, Milan

1971

Artemide showroom, Milan

1972

House at Barzana, Bergamo

1973
—

● Hotel Restaurant Locanda dell'Angelo, Ameglia, Sarzana
House at Varese
MBM prefabricated Buildings, Ca' Granda Sud District, Milan

1974

House at Portobello di Gallura
Renovation of furnished apartment building in via Borgonuovo, Milan
Buitoni-France offices, Paris
Cerruti, showroom, Tokyo
Schiffini store, La Spezia
Meda Sud primary school (with Gae Aulenti)
New Vanak district, Teheran (with L. and G. Barsanti)

1975

Houses at San Quirico, Brunello, Varese

1976

Houses at Rocca Llisa, Ibiza (with F. Soro)
Schiffini store, Rome
Lanerossi office renovation, Arezzo
Lanerossi office and showroom renovation, Milan
Cerruti showroom, Teheran

1977

● Secondary School, San Daniele del Friuli
Schiffini store, Milan
Cerruti showroom, Vienna

1978	Department of Biology, Università Statale, Milan (with F. Soro)

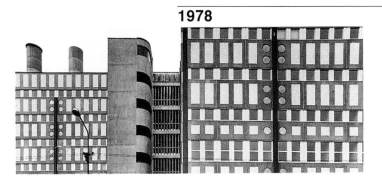

1979	Cassina showroom, Milan
1982	House at Marina di Massa
1985	• Centro Cavagnari Cassa di Risparmio di Parma, Parma Clubhouse of Castelconturbia Golf Club, Agrate Castelconturbia (with Studio Beta) Renotavion of house in via Gesù 10, Milan

1986	• House in Tokyo Cerruti showroom, Osaka Cerruti showroom, London

1987	Tecnocentro Cassa di Risparmio di Bologna, Bologna Seaside house, Aburatsubo, Japan
1988	Second renovation of furnished apartment building in via Borgonuovo, Milan
1989	MM Famagosta subway deposit, Milan

1990	Barilla offices, second project, Parma

DESIGNS IN PUBLIC COLLECTIONS

MUSEUM OF MODERN ART, NEW YORK
Demetrio table
Eclisse lamp
Cirene lamp
Stadio table
Giunone lamp
Selene lamp
Gaudi armchair
Vicario armchair
Maralunga armchair and sofa
Atollo lamp
Veranda armchair
Silver cutlery, Cleto Munari

METROPOLITAN MUSEUM OF ART, NEW YORK
Vicario armchair

VICTORIA AND ALBERT MUSEUM, LONDON
Maralunga armchair and sofa
Veranda armchair

PHILADELPHIA MUSEUM OF ART
Atollo lamp

KUNSTGEWERBEMUSEUM, ZURICH
Atollo lamp

MUSEUM DIE NEUE SAMMLUNG, MUNICH
Atollo lamp
Snow lamp
Slalom lamp

MUSEUM FUR KUNST UND GEWERBE, HAMBURG
Atollo lamp
Kuta lamp
Idomeneo lamp

MUSEUM FUR ANGEWANDTE KUNST, COLOGNE
Atollo lamp
Slalom lamp
Lester lamp

KUNSTMUSEUM, DUSSELDORF
Atollo lamp

JEWISH MUSEUM, NEW YORK
Golem chair

CONRAN MUSEUM, LONDON
Sindbad armchair

DESIGN — AUSWAHL, STUTTGART
Lester lamp

SOUTHWEST MUSEUM OF SCIENCE AND TECHNOLOGY, DALLAS
Spiros clothes-tree

KUNSTINDUSTRIMUSEET (MUSEUM OF DECORATIVE ARTS), COPENHAGEN
Vidun table
Babe table

LIST OF DESIGNS

1946
Bookcase and chair, Moretti
• Folding canvas armchair, RIMA exhibition
Bookcase, RIMA exhibition
Single bedroom, RIMA exhibition
Desk
Dining or gaming table
Bookcase for leaning against the wall
Claritas lamp

1949
Stackable tables, Azucena
Coatstand
Office unit

1951
Extendable round *Sending I* table, Azucena

1960
Carimate 892 chair with arms, Cassina
Amaja

1961
Carimate 115 chair, Cassina
928 armchair, Cassina
113 bed, Cassina
Omicron lamp, Artemide
Loden armchair, Gavina

1962

930 armchair, Cassina
122 chair, Cassina
Lambda lamp, Artemide
Caori occasional table, Gavina

1963

896 armchair, Cassina
772 table, Cassina
897 armchair, Cassina
Omega lamp, Artemide
Clinio lamp, Artemide
Triclinio lamp, Artemide
Pentaclinio lamp, Artemide
Eptaclinio lamp, Artemide
Erse lamp, Artemide
Clitumno lamp, Artemide
Mania lamp, Artemide

1964

905 armchair, Cassina
912 bed, Cassina
913 bed, Cassina
764 stackable tables, Cassina
Cetra lamp, Artemide
Demetrio 45 and *Demetrio 70* tables, Artemide

1965

Dalù lamp, Artemide
● *Eclisse* lamp, Artemide
Cirene lamp, Artemide
Vejo handle, Artemide
781 table, Cassina
764 table base, Cassina
921 armchair, Cassina
922 armchair, Cassina

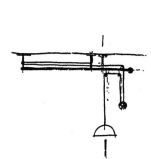

1966

Chimera lamp, Artemide
Mezzachimera lamp, Artemide
Arcadia occasional table, Artemide
Elena occasional table, Artemide
Stadio table, Artemide
Telegono lamp, Artemide
Tessera table, Artemide
Mezzatessera occasional table, Artemide
Carimate 927 chair, Cassina

1967

Teti lamp, Artemide
Triteti lamp, Artemide
937 cupboard-ladder-bed, Cassina

1968

Caledonia armchair, C&B Italia

1969

Giunione lamp, Artemide
Ecatombe lamp, Artemide
Selene chair, Artemide
Samarcanda chest of drawers, Poggi

1970

Gaudì armchair, Artemide
Vicario armchair, Artemide
● *Impiccato* lamp, Artemide
Lyndon lamp, Oluce
Golem chair, Poggi

1972

Flower vase, Bacci
Open armchair, B&B Italia
Tema, Sestetto, Quartetto, Mezzacoda tables, B&B
Siloe sofa-bed, T 70
Occasional table and lamp, Krupp
Timo kitchen line, Schiffini

1973	*Maralunga* armchair and sofa, Cassina *Snow* lamp, Oluce
1974	*Sonora* lamp, Oluce *Ring* lamp, Oluce *Palmer* occasional table, Poggi *Campiglia* table, Schiffini
1975	*Ekkon* lamp, Oluce *Selavy* armchair, OCA Brasil *Armilla* lamp, Artemide *Troco* lamp, Artemide *Fiandra* armchair, Cassina *908, 909, 910* chairs, Montina *911, 914, 915, 918, 919* tables, Montina *913* bed, Montina *912* cupboard, Montina
1976	*Porsenna* lamp, Artemide *Ribbon* armchair, Asko *Tenorio* armchair, Asko *Safram* chair, Asko *Safram mini* chair, Asko *Savana* chair, Asko *Tay Argento* office furniture, ICF *Dim* lamp, Oluce • *Adim* lamp, Oluce *Linz* lamp, Oluce *Dama* kitchen line, Schiffini
1977	• *Nuvola rossa* bookcase, Cassina *Atollo* lamp, Oluce *Albatros* lamp, Oluce *Alida* lamp, Oluce *Kalaari* lamp, Oluce *Orsola* lamp, Vistosi
1978	*Marienbad* bathroom units, Carrara e Matta *Nathalie* bed, Flou *Alega* lamp, Vistosi *Davis* office chair, ICF *Lobby* office armchair, ICF *Melilla* lamp, Oluce *Kuta* lamp, Oluce *Boboli* lamp, Superior
1979	*Nemea* lamp, Artemide *Dui* lamp, Artemide *Regina d'Africa* armchair, Alias *Tanganika* chair, Alias *Tenorio* coat stand, Alias *Bath* bookcase, Alias *Gobi* table, Alias *Kilim* table, Alias *Clam* bed, De Padova *Pascal* lamp, Oluce *Tanganika* chair, Alias
1980	*Cap* sofa, Alias *Paddock* sofa, Cassina *Andrej* bed, Flou *Monet* lamp, Oluce *Nara* lamp, Oluce *Barbettis* chair, Poggi • *Silver* cutlery, Cleto Munari *Pan* chair, Rosenthal *Pan set* table, Rosenthal *Genius loci* kitchen line, Schiffini

1981	• *Sindbad* armchair and sofa, Cassina *Sindbad* occasional table, Cassina Bedside table, Flou *Faun* chair and table, Rosenthal Golf bag, Spalding
1983	*Veranda* sofa and armchair, Cassina *Veranda* occasional table, Cassina *Bengalka* chair, Alias *Kobe* bed, De Padova
1984	*Veranda 3* sofa, Cassina *Simi* chair, Alias
1985	*Villabianca* chair with arms, Cassina *Edison* table, Cassina *G 12* sofa and armchair, Gervasoni *Pianeta* lamp, Venini *Cina* lamp, Oluce *Idomeneo* lamp, Oluce *Slalom* lamp, Oluce
1986	*Cardigan* armchair and sofa, Cassina *Koube* chair, Aidec Tokyo *Vidun* table, De Padova *Leone 1°* bed, Flou *Ermellino* bed, Flou *4 M* series handles, Fusital *Roskis* occasional table, Messin Finland *Idomedue* lamp, Oluce *Morgan* writing desk, ICF
1987	• *Marocca* chair, De Padova *Express* sofa, De Padova *Timótei* bed, Messin Finland *Siam* lamp, Oluce *Lester* lamp, Oluce *Spiros* clothes-tree, Acerbis *Leone III* bed, Flou *Ping-pong* party dish, John Cook, London Table decoration, Ultima Edizione
1988	Handles for the *Tipo*, Fiat Auto *Shigeto* cupboard, De Padova *Babe 1°, 2°, 3°* tables, De Padova *Raffles* armchair, De Padova Re-edition of chair, Montina *35* kitchen line, Schiffini *Simi* chair, Aidec Tokyo
1989	*Silver* chair, De Padova *Reflex* chest of drawers, De Padova *Florian* folding occasional tables, Acerbis • *Portovenere* armchair, Cassina *Hotel* lamp, Oluce *Fleo* occasional table, Acerbis *India* bed, Flou
1990	Flower vase, Cleto Munari *Spigo 1-2-3-4* bedside table, chest of drawers, chest, Flou *Shime* occasional table, De Padova *La Serra* sofa, De Padova *Ribbon* bed, De Padova *Susanna* armchair, De Padova *Rocking* pouff, De Padova *Campiglia* kitchen, Schiffini *Spiros 2* clothes-tree, Acerbis *Kalea* lamp, Artemide *Hotel 402* lamp, Oluce

BIBLIOGRAPHY

Albera, G., Monti, N., *Italian Modern — A Design Heritage* (New York, 1989).

Ambasz, E., editor, *Italy: The New Domestic Landscape* (Florence, 1972).

Bangert, A., *Italienisches mobeldesign* (Munich, 1985).

Baroni, D., *L'oggetto lampada* (Milan, 1981).

Bayley, S., *The Conran Directory of Design* (London, 1985).

Bellini, M., editor, *The International Design Yearbook 1990–1* (London, 1990).

Bonfanti, E., Porta, M., *Città, Museo e Architettura* (Florence, 1973).

Bosoni, G., Confalonieri, F., *Paesaggio del design italiano 1972–1988* (Milan, 1988).

Capella, J., Larrea, Q., *Diseño de arquitectos en los 80* (Barcelona, 1987).

Compasso d'Oro 1954–1984 (Milan, 1985).

De Fusco, R., *Storia del design* (Milan, 1985).

Descendants of Leonardo da Vinci — The Italian Design (Tokyo, 1987).

Design als Postulat am Beispiel Italien (Berlin, 1973).

Fischer, V., editor, *Design heute* (Munich, 1988).

Frateili, E., *Il disegno industriale italiano. 1928–1981* (Turin, 1983).

——, *Continuità e trasformazione: Una storia del design italiano, 1928–1988* (Milan, 1989).

Giacomoni, S., Marcolli, A., *Designer italiani* (Milan, 1988).

Gramigna, G., *1959–1980: Repertorio* (Milan, 1985).

Grassi, A., Pansera, A., *L'Italia del design* (Casale Monferrato, 1986).

Gregotti, V., *Il disegno del prodotto industriale: Italia 1860–1980* (Milan, 1982).

Habegger, Y., Osman, J., *Sourcebook of Modern Furniture* (New York, 1989).

Isozaki, A., editor, *The International Design Yearbook 1988–9* (London, 1988).

Italia diseño 1946–1986 (Bosque de Chapultepec, Mexico, 1986).

Lavrillier, M., *50 designers dal 1950 al 1975* (Novara, 1978).

Mang, K., *Geschichte des modernen Möbels* (Stuttgart, 1978).

Mastropietro, M., editor, *Un'industria per il design* (Milan, 1982).

Pansera, A., *Storia e cronaca della Triennale* (Milan, 1978).

——, *Il design del mobile italiano dal 1946 ad oggi* (Bari, 1990).

Raimondi, G., *Abitare Italia — La cultura dell'arredamento in trent'anni di storia italiana* (Milan, 1988).

Sabino, C., Tondini, A., *Italian Style* (London, 1985).

Santini, P. C., *Gli anni del design italiano — Ritratto di Cesare Cassina* (Milan, 1981).

Sparke, P., *Design in Context* (London, 1987).

——, *Italian Design* (London, 1988).

Wichmann, H., *Industrial design — Unikate Serienerzeugnisse* (Munich, 1985).

——, *Italien: Design 1945 bis heute* (Munich, 1988).

Wills, G., Baroni, D., Chiarelli, B., *Il mobile — storia progettisti tipi e stili* (Milan, 1983).

BIOGRAPHY

Vico Magistretti was born in Milan, where he took a degree in architecture in 1945. Since 1967 he has been a member of the Academy of San Luca in Rome. In 1951 he won the gold medal at the IX Triennale; in 1954 the foremost award at the X Triennale; in 1967 and 1979 the Compasso d'Oro; in 1986 the S.I.A.D. (Society of Industrial Artists and Designers) gold medal. He is an honorary member of the Royal College of Art in London and of the Royal Incorporation of Architects in Scotland. His works have been exhibited in the principal design shows held in Italy, Europe, the United States and Japan; they are also kept in the permanent collections of the world's most important museums. He has held conferences in Milan, Venice, Rome, London, Barcelona, Copenhagen, Aspen, Tokyo, and San Paolo. He has taught at Domus Academy in Milan, and is Honorary Visiting Professor at the Royal College of Art in London.